C000045764

A BETTER WAY

Simon Austen writes as a gifted preacher, desiring to explain the message of the Bible as a whole and to show how the Lord Jesus Christ is the key to unlock its meaning. In a sense, each chapter is a gospel presentation, with a different starting-point in the Old Testament, but always leading us to Christ. It is a helpful model for preachers and other Bible teachers and could also be used as the basis for a home-group study course. I warmly commend it.

David Peterson, Principal
Oakhill College, London

Once again we must thank Simon Austen for writing clearly and compellingly – and with a welcome regard for the capacities of a wide-ranging readership. *A Better Way* brings us an attractive survey of the Christ-centred truths running right through the Scriptures. It will have a happy appeal for the new and enthusiastic generation of Bible students that we now see emerging world-wide. Equally it will bring clarification and fresh stimulation into the arena of preachers, Bible class leaders and theological seminars.

Richard Bewes, Rector
All Souls Church, Langham Place, London

This is a superb, engagingly written and immensely timely book. Without burying you in the jargon of professional theologians, Simon Austen, carefully, clearly and with astute sensitivity to the text of the Scriptures, brings alive the tragically forgotten territory of the Old Testament's fulfilment in Christ. Reading this book, your understanding of the great salvation that we have in Christ will deepen, Christ will be exalted in your mind and heart, and your assurance of God's work for you in him will strengthen.

We desperately need this kind of biblical theology. Read it, and give a copy to anyone in your church who handles the word of God!

Dominic Smart, Pastor
Gilcomston South Church of Scotland, Aberdeen

A BETTER WAY

SIMON AUSTEN

JESUS AND OLD TESTAMENT FULFILMENT

CHRISTIAN FOCUS PUBLICATIONS

All rights reserved. No part of this publication may be reproduced, stored in a retrieval system, or transmitted, in any form, by any means, electronic, mechanical, photocopying, recording or otherwise without the prior permission of the publisher or a licence permitting restricted copying. In the U.K. such licences are issued by the Copyright Licensing Agency, 90 Tottenham Court Road, London W1P 9HE.

Scripture quotations are taken from The Holy Bible, New International Version © 1973, 1978, 1984 by International Bible Society. Used by permission.

ISBN 1-85792-867-9

© Copyright Simon Austen 2003

Published in 2003
by
Christian Focus Publications, Ltd
Geanies House, Fearn, Tain,
Ross-shire, IV20 1TW, Great Britain.

www.christianfocus.com

Cover design by Alister MacInnes

Printed and bound by
Cox & Wyman, Ltd, Reading, Berkshire

'No matter how many promises God has made,
they are "yes" in Christ'

2 Corinthians 1:20

CONTENTS

Introduction

In the eighteenth century Voltaire said that 200 years later there would not be a Bible left on earth. He was wrong. The Bible remains a world best seller. And yet for most of us it is a closed book, clothed in the language of the sixteenth century, feared, neglected, misunderstood and little read. The Old Testament in particular is foreign territory. It seems alien, barbaric, uncivilized and mythical. The little knowledge we do have comes from memories of the stories we learnt at school or Sunday school – Noah and his ark, Moses crossing the Red Sea, Daniel in the Lion's den . . . . But now we have abandoned it. Some have forgotten it and increasingly few have any knowledge of its contents, let alone any understanding of what it means. On one end of the spectrum, liberal scholarship has undermined the confidence of those who regard themselves as intellectually rigorous, and on the other end of the spectrum, stories of judgement have been twisted into fanciful tales for children, with money-making spin-offs for the toy industry.

In our schools, few pupils have any knowledge of those dim and distant days of the Bible. In my days as a school chaplain I would sometimes start a lesson by drawing a line across the board with 'Genesis' written at one end and 'Revelation' written at the other, asking the class to fill in any details they knew. Someone might mention two testaments; another might place Jesus hesitantly on the right hand side of the board. After a pause there might be an attempt to write 'Moses' somewhere in the middle of the Old. Then others would call out . . . David, Adam . . . before silence fell once again. Slowly they realised how little they knew.

Even Christians are confused. Kitchen calendar verses leave us with blessed thoughts from Proverbs or words of woe and lamentation ripped out of context to set us up for the day. Some leave the Old Testament behind, convinced that the God of the New Testament is more loving, less angry and generally nicer to know.

But the Jesus we call Lord might cause us to think differently. When he spoke to the religious leaders of the day he reminded them that the scriptures they so diligently studied – the Old Testament as we now have it – were all about him. It wasn't a book to be neglected, but equally it wasn't a book which should be misunderstood. It was and is a book about Jesus.

It wasn't only his religious opponents who had missed the point. His own friends were bewildered and confused because they had failed to understand the scriptures. Luke tells us that they had 'hoped he was the one who was going to redeem Israel.' But their hopes were dashed in the agony of the crucifixion. Then shortly afterwards, while still in shock, they met a man on the way to Emmaus – no ordinary man, but the risen Lord Jesus, his identity hidden as they walked along the road. As he heard their uncertain attempts to make sense of his death, he said to them, "'How foolish you are, and how slow of heart to believe all that the prophets have written! Did not the Christ have to suffer these things and then enter his glory?" And beginning with Moses and all the Prophets, he explained to them what was said in all the Scriptures concerning himself' (Luke 24:25-27). Jesus was handing the Old Testament back to his confused disciples with the simple message 'it is about me.'

This book is a gentle attempt to give the Old Testament back to everyday Christians in just the same way. It is not a theological text book, but rather an applied tour of the Bible, showing how its message is all about Jesus. My hope is that it will give renewed confidence in that most famous of all books – and as we have renewed confidence may we also have a renewed relationship with the one of whom it speaks.

1

A Better Adam

One of the delights and amusements of having children is the well-meant comments from others about one's assorted offspring. Family friends and relatives look lovingly into the eyes of the young and say 'you are just like your father' (or mother, as the case may be). As a father I smile, not only because I remember the same being said of me when I was a child, but also because I wonder exactly what is meant. Does my child look like me? Do any positive qualities come to mind? Is it that as an adult, this dear old friend knows what I am really like and sees my true character reflected in my child? Does that 'where's my present?' look of my son or daughter reflect the selfish attitude with which I battle?

As we begin to think about it, our lives and characters are all very mixed. We don't have to be parents too long before we realize the raw reality of human nature. Children can be delightful and they can be obnoxious. Children can be kind and generous and they can be incredibly selfish.

The only difference between them and us is that we have learnt the social framework to mask our greed, our selfishness, our arrogance and our folly. But our hearts are no better and our motives no more pure. We are like our children and they are like us – human. And innate in humanity is a sinfulness that not so much *runs to* the very core of who we are, but *comes from* that very core and pervades everything we do. Only when we understand the Bible do we see where sin comes from and how it can be dealt with.

Scripture speaks of two Adams. We find one at the beginning of the Old Testament and one at the beginning of the New Testament. The first is the Adam of creation and the second Adam, or 'last' Adam is Jesus of Nazareth.

> The first man Adam became a living being; the last Adam, a life giving spirit . . . The first man was of the dust of the earth, the second man from heaven. (1 Corinthians 15:45,47)

These two Adams give explanation and identity to the human race and give shape to the Bible. They explain why we are as we are and what can be done about it. All of us will not only identify with one or other of these figures, but Biblically speaking, we will be a part of them.

The first Adam – Perfection to Pollution

> God created man in his own image, in the image of God he created him; male and female he created them. God blessed them and said to them, 'Be fruitful and increase in number; fill the earth and subdue it. Rule over the fish of the sea and the birds of the air and over every living creature that moves on the ground.' (Genesis 1:27,28)

Adam was created in the image of God to rule over creation and care for it. There was and is something distinct about humankind which makes us different from the animals. Adam was God's vice-regent, a privileged caretaker who had direct communion with God. The

New Testament even goes so far as to call him 'the Son of God.'[1] It was a perfect relationship. Mankind enjoyed the presence and company of God in surroundings where there was nothing but beauty, harmony and order.

But Adam fell into temptation and sin. The one request from God was that he must not eat from the tree of the knowledge of good and evil, for if he did, he would die. Death would be the result of wanting to be 'like God' (Genesis 3:5). And that 'being like God' was and is expressed in disobedience. Rather than submitting to the creator and living within his loving framework of relationship, the created set himself up in opposition to the creator. When Adam took the forbidden fruit he made a bid for divine status, opting to decide for himself what was morally right and morally wrong. As he did so he brought the judgement of God on the whole of humanity. The raw reality of human nature finds its origins in the Garden of Eden.

That one event had a greater and more profound effect on the human race than any other event in history. The birth of Hitler or Stalin had a devastating effect on the lives of millions and changed the course of history, but although they affected countless individuals, both directly and indirectly, relatively few people now suffer the consequence of their actions; The decision to allow the Challenger shuttle to take off in freezing conditions in 1986 against the advice of engineers led to death and tragedy and world-wide shock, but again, very few remain personally bereaved; The temporary loss of binoculars on the look-out of the Titanic on 15th April 1912 and the decision to go full-ahead in waters strewn with icebergs led to the tragic death of 1500 people – but now it touches most of us only in the guise of entertainment and historical interest. Political decisions, public and private decisions about use of money and time, the concerns of what we do, when and with whom we do it, all have an influence on the lives of others, to a lesser or greater extent. But no decision affected history as much as the decision of Adam in the Garden of Eden.

When Adam disobeyed God by eating the forbidden fruit the whole of the created order changed. The corporate identity of mankind became a shadow of what it was created to be. Through one act of disobedience you and I became rebels against God. My sin was and is because of Adam's sin. It is not simply that I am like him, prone to sin, imitating his rebellion. The Bible tells me that his sin is the cause of my sinfulness. When Adam rebelled against God he took me with him. I don't simply imitate the sin of Adam, I participate in it. We all do.

> . . . sin entered the world through one man, and
> death through sin, and in this way death came to
> all men, because all sinned. (Romans 5:12)

And just as the consequence of Adam's sin was expulsion from God's presence, a curse and a godless death, so it is for us. The New Testament tells me that 'All have sinned and fallen short of the glory of God.' (Romans 3:23). Adam's rebellion explains my rebellion and the judgement of God that befell him is the judgement of God that befalls me.

Yet in the midst of the curse that fell on Adam, Eve and the serpent, we find a promise. There in the ashes of despair we find a spark of hope. An offspring of Eve will crush the serpent. (i.e Satan)[2]

> And I will put enmity between you and the woman,
> and between your offspring and hers; he will crush
> your head, and you will strike his heel.' (Genesis
> 3:15)

God will restore paradise. Satan (the serpent) will be
destroyed. The Old Testament awaits a second Adam,
an offspring of Eve, who will rescue us from the actions
of the first.

The Second Adam – Polluted for Perfection

One of the descriptions given to Jesus in the New
Testament is 'the last Adam.' Like the first Adam, Jesus
is also described as 'The Son of God.' It would be very
difficult to read any one of the four gospels without being
left with a clear sense that Jesus fits that description. In
Matthew, Mark and Luke, Jesus' ministry begins with a
heavenly declaration as to his identity. 'This is my Son,
whom I love.'[3] And as his ministry begins, Satan and
his minions are the first to spot the arrival of the second
Adam. He tempts Jesus to show his true sonship as he
presents him with attractive and identity-proving options
in the desert: 'If you are the Son of God, tell these stones
to become bread.' (Matthew 4:3). But Jesus would not
have it. For unlike the first Adam, Jesus did not submit
to the serpent's lies. 'He committed no sin, and no deceit
was found in his mouth.' (1 Peter 2:22)

Rather than submit to Satan, Jesus came to crush him.
He was the long-awaited offspring of Eve. That is why
Luke is so keen to make the connection. After the
familiar Christmas stories of the birth of the saviour
king, Luke then traces the ancestry of Jesus back to Adam
(and therefore Eve) so that we would understand that
the promised Satan crusher has arrived.[4] And as if to

make is doubly clear, we find Luke's account of the temptations of Jesus in the verses that follow. Satan may have won the loyalty of the first Adam, but he was powerless to rule the second. Jesus, the sinless Son of God, was the only man since Adam to live without being under the authority of Satan. His mission would take him to the cross so that Satan could be defeated and Eden restored. Jesus, the second Adam, in being the sinless man, was uniquely qualified to deal with the actions and consequences of the first.

So as we open the scriptures and begin to read, Jesus of Nazareth is already standing on the horizon. 'Where Adam stands at the beginning of human history, we see Jesus Christ. He is the son, bearing the image of his father. He overcomes in temptation and his sonship is proved in obedience.'[5] It is this second Adam who shows a better service, giving us a better gift and taking us to a better destiny.

A better service

When Adam took the forbidden fruit, he was serving no one but himself. The garden was beautiful and perfect. He had a wonderful wife and a tremendous relationship with God. Serving others would have been relatively easy. But instead he served himself. He made the choice to disobey God for no other reason than he was tempted to do so – the fruit 'was pleasing to the eye and also desirable for gaining wisdom.' (Genesis 3:6)

But to the same degree that Adam was self-serving, Jesus, the second Adam, was selfless and self-sacrificial. He did not live in Eden, where all was harmony and perfection. He lived in the fallen world of the selfish and the self-serving – the world as we know it today.

And yet it was in that world and for that world that he gave himself, forfeiting on the cross a perfect relationship with his heavenly Father. Jesus sacrificed himself and was cut off from God so that the world – you and me – would not suffer the consequences of our selfishness but rather experience a renewed relationship with God himself.

> Consequently, just as the result of one trespass was condemnation for all men, so also the result of one act of righteousness was justification that brings life for all men. (Romans 5:18)

Where Adam was selfish and self-seeking, Jesus was selfless.

A better gift

> Again, the gift of God is not like the result of one man's sin: The judgement followed one sin and brought condemnation, but the gift followed many trespasses and brought justification. (Romans 5:16)

Adam's one sin brought condemnation on humanity. Because of the judgement on him, judgement also hangs over you and me. But I don't only participate in the sin of Adam, I also repeat it. Any look at the world and any honest account of our own lives will show that we sin. Therefore I am not only under condemnation because of what Adam did, but also because of what I continue to do. Adam was unrighteous. So am I.

But unlike Adam and me, Jesus was righteous. As I look at Adam I may know *why* I sin – but it does not stop me from sinning. I cannot hold my head up and say that I am innocent. My sin rightly deserves to be punished by a righteous God. I have rebelled against the creator. And yet although I am deserving of his judgement, God offers me his love. Nothing I have done warrants such an outpouring of grace. There is nothing in my life which makes me worthy of the selfless act of self-substitution on the cross. My sin should have nailed me, the guilty one, to the tree of Calvary, not Jesus. Yet where I expect condemnation, I find mercy.

So if I cry out at the apparent injustice of my inclusion in the sin of Adam I should also cry over my inclusion in the righteousness of Jesus. Indeed, perhaps I should cry out at the injustice of the love of God – for the gift far outweighs the crime. It is disproportionate. Such is the love and grace of God. The gift of his death means that I can be justified, made right with God – though I deserve nothing but his condemnation.

A better destiny

Adam's sin led to the spiritual death of humanity. It means that my ultimate destiny will be eternal death unless I respond to Jesus. Only in Christ can I be made alive. Through him I can have new life now and real life beyond the grave.

> For if, by the trespass of the one man, death reigned through that one man, how much more will those who receive God's abundant provision of grace and of the gift of righteousness reign in life through the one man, Jesus Christ. (Romans 5:17)

I may feel it unjust that I am caught up in Adam's sin; after all I was not there when Adam sinned. But I still sin and deserve its consequence. Equally, I was not there when Christ died and likewise I don't deserve the consequence of what his death brings for me – a glorious and eternal future with God. It is a tremendous privilege that although by birth I may be in Adam, by re-birth I can be in Christ.

'Look at yourself in Adam; though you had done nothing you were declared a sinner. Look at yourself in Christ; and see that, though you have done nothing, you are declared to be righteous. That is the parallel.'[6]

Praise to the holiest in the height
And in the depth be praise:
In all his words most wonderful,
Most sure in all his ways.

O loving wisdom of our God!
When all was sin and shame
A second Adam to the fight,
And to the rescue came.

O wisest love! That flesh and blood
Which did in Adam fail,
Should strive afresh against the foe,
Should strive and should prevail.

NOTES:

[1] Luke 3:38

[2] In the book of Revelation, Satan is spoken of as a serpent (Revelation 12:9; 20:2)

[3] Matthew 3:17; Mark 1:11; Luke 3:22

[4] Luke 3:23-37

[5] Edmund Clowney *The Unfolding Mystery* (Navipress, 1988) p.35

[6] Martyn Lloyd-Jones. *Romans* (Banner of Truth Trust) Vol. 4 (Assurance) 1971 p.274

2

A Better Son

Edward Gibbon said 'history is little more than the register of the crimes, follies and misfortunes of mankind.' He could well have said the same of the Old Testament. When Adam and Eve left the garden they forfeited much of what was good and everything that was perfect. Thereafter we have little more than a register of the crimes, follies and misfortunes of fallen humanity – the fruit of mankind's rebellion in the garden. The chapters that follow this 'fall', (Genesis 3-11), 'disclose the hopeless plight of mankind . . . an avalanche of sin that gradually engulfs, leading first to mankind's near annihilation in the flood and second to man's dispersal over the face of earth in despair of achieving international co-operation.'[1]

Yet through it all we hear the words of God's promise in the garden faintly calling from the midst of the curse of Genesis 3. God will crush the serpent (Satan), he will restore the problem through an offspring of Eve. It is just that we can't see how – Cain murders his brother Abel in chapter 4; sexual perversion reaches its peak in chapter 6 before the flood brings a watery chaos to God's creation. Even Noah, so honourable and righteous, is later caught up in the sin of his own drunkenness, resulting in a curse that created the enemies of Israel.

And finally in the tower of Babel, we witness the world's pathetic attempt to reach heaven. For eight chapters of Genesis and generations of Eve's descendants we see nothing but the muck and mess of sin. Left to their own devices, God's distorted creatures have little hope of restoring the relationship with God.

The problem they had is the problem we have. We can't get it right. However hard we try, it is simply impossible to deal with sin and restore our relationship with God. Only a divine initiative could remedy the problem. An action of God was required. And that is exactly what happened.

Abraham – A powerful Patriarch

It all seemed very unlikely. On the surface Abram and Sarai were no more than a man and wife who lived with their extended family and struggled with the pain of childlessness. But then God spoke.

> The Lord had said to Abram, 'Leave your country, your people and your father's household and go to the land I will show you.
>
> I will make you into a great nation and I will bless you;
>
> I will make your name great, and you will be a blessing.
>
> I will bless those who bless you, and whoever curses you I will curse;
>
> And all peoples on earth will be blessed through you.' (Genesis 12:1-3)

Only a chapter before these great words do we read of the futile attempt of the world to make a city with a tower that reached to the heavens. They desired to 'make a name for [themselves] and not be scattered over the face of the whole earth.' (Genesis 11:4). But as with every attempt in history to challenge the sovereign Lord, they found themselves overruled by his might and power. They were scattered throughout the earth, with no great tower and no great name. Only God would have worldwide dominion and only God would make mankind great again. It was to be through an individual, not a nation, that a great name would be made and blessings would flow to the world.

So God spoke to Abram and made a promise to an individual that would have ramifications for the whole world. There was no great tower or city, just a great God and one trusting man. Through him all nations of the world would be blessed. Humanly speaking, it was extraordinary. Abram was a seventy-five year old man with no children – he had no offspring from whom a nation could be created. There was nothing obvious to suggest that this man and the promise given to him would be the bedrock on which the work of God in reconciling mankind to himself would be built. In fact, 'All natural events seem to work against the fulfilment of the promise.'[2]

Abram would have known this better than anyone. He was old and he was childless – everything he knew about himself suggested that this promise was unreal and unrealistic. But because it was God who had made the promise, 'Abram left, as the LORD had told him.' (Genesis 12:4)

And so a foundation stone was laid – not only for the activity of God in the Old Testament, but a foundation stone on which every Christian in the world today now stands. Abram's story would determine the history of the world, through a promised people, a promised land and, most importantly, a promised seed.

A promised people

It must have been quite a shock when God told Abram that he would make him into a great nation and bless him. Most men of seventy-five look back on their lives and careers with mixed emotions. They reminisce about the sleepless nights of early parenthood, of wise and not-so-wise decisions they have made at work and in the home. They smile at the fun and innocence of their children's children. Their own families and homes have scaled down in size and the wider family now absorbs their interest and their time. After all, there may only be a few years left. But Abram was different. All this was ahead of him. God said:

> 'A son coming from your own body will be your heir.' He took him outside and said 'Look up to the heavens and count the stars – if indeed you can count them.' Then he said 'So shall your offspring be.'
> (Genesis 15:4b,5)

A child from his own body would be the start of this great nation. As he went home that night he must have looked at his beloved Sarai and wondered how it would happen. She was an old lady and long ago they would have abandoned their shared hope of a child to succeed them and with it the removal of the social stigma of childlessness. Abram probably didn't know how it would happen. But God had spoken and so Abram believed him and it was 'credited to him as righteousness.' (Genesis 15:6)

In that one act of faith Abram not only received the promise of a future people of faith but provided a model for all people of true faith – for humanly there was nothing to suggest that the promise could be realized. Abram was in just the same situation before God as we are. Humanly we have nothing to commend ourselves to God. All that we do, all the good we attempt, all the religion we pursue will not make us right before a holy God. We are as spiritually weak as Abram was physically unable to sire a child. But God had made a promise to Abram, and Abram believed him. That was enough for him. It should be enough for us too. God has taken the initiative to reconcile us to him in the death and resurrection of his son. We contribute nothing but our sin to that once for all act of reconciliation – in and of ourselves we are as far from achieving righteousness before God as Abram was of fathering a nation. Our right standing before God is achieved by God alone – all we have to do is to believe. It means that the words we read in Genesis are more than words about Abraham and for Abraham. They are words for us:

> The words 'it was credited to him' were written not for him alone, but also for us, to whom God will credit righteousness – for us who believe in him who raised Jesus our Lord from the dead. (Romans 4:23,24)

So Abram was to be the father of a great nation. But as with so much of the Old Testament, it wasn't straightforward. The years rolled by and Sarai still had not conceived – her womb was 'as good as dead.' In desperation she suggested a plan to take away her shame and start a family. Abram could father a child through Sarai's maid, Hagar. In the ancient world such practice was quite common and in many ways it seemed quite sensible – God hadn't specified how the nation would be formed. Maybe it was through Hagar? Abram accepted the idea and Hagar conceived.

Some would say that Abram doubted God's promise, but I am not so sure. Although Sarai laughed at the prospect of having a child, perhaps through fear or disbelief (Genesis 18:13-15), the New Testament tells us that Abram 'did not waver through unbelief regarding the promise of God, but was strengthened in his faith and gave glory to God, being fully persuaded that God had power to do what he had promised.' (Romans 4:20,21). Abram did not know *how* the promise would be fulfilled, but he trusted God that it *would be* fulfilled. He would never have imagined just how gracious and good God would be – for it was not to be through Hagar but through Sarai that the promise would be fulfilled and the great nation created.

And so the promise of God reached its climax. Abram was to change his name to Abraham, the father of many. Sarai was to change her name to Sarah as the mark of the promise God had made. From the two of them many nations, even kings, would come. The promise would be eternal – a great people, God's people, would come from this elderly, childless couple.

Immediately Abraham responded by circumcising himself and those in his household – a strong and brave sign that he believed God's promise. He was now 100 years old and Sarah was 90. Once he knew how the nation would begin, his faith did not waver. And a year later their son, Isaac, was born.

A promised Land

It wasn't just a great nation that God promised Abram. He also promised a great land. God's people would once again be in God's place under God's blessing. Perhaps Abram found it too much – he had just been told that his descendants would be as numerous as the stars in the sky and now he was being told that God would give them the land in which he was now living. This was a promise to beat all promises. No wonder Abram asked the Lord, 'How can I know that I shall gain possession of it?' (Genesis 15:8)

The way in which God confirmed his promise is rather alien to the modern mind. When we make agreements with one another we sign a contract or shake a hand. Lawyers and legal structures are used to keep us to our word. There is a cost involved if we break our contract – often financially and almost always personally.

In the ancient world contracts were equally binding, but the way in which they were confirmed was quite different. Once the agreement or 'covenant' was written up it was often 'signed' by sacrifice. An animal would be cut in two and the two halves would be placed a distance apart. Each party of the agreement would then walk through the two pieces of the sacrifice as a kind of visual aid. The message was 'if you don't keep your side of the bargain, what has happened to this animal will happen to you – and if I don't keep my side of the bargain, what has happened to this animal will happen to me.' It was a very clear way of making the agreement binding and a sobering reminder of what would happen if the agreement, or covenant, was broken.

Here in Genesis, God confirms his promise to Abram in a similar way. He instructs Abram to take a heifer, a

goat and a ram, along with a dove and a young pigeon.
Abram cuts them in two and arranges the halves opposite
each other. We would then expect God and Abram, as
representatives of the two sides of the promise, to walk
between the pieces. Only that doesn't happen. Instead
Abram falls into a deep sleep and a smoking brazier with
a blazing torch passes between the pieces. God alone
has bound himself to this promise. He will keep it on
pain of his own death. Abram, on the other hand, has
no part to play.

The promise is then reiterated over the next few
chapters. God will give a land to his people in which
they will be blessed. For a childless nomad, this was
undeserved generosity – and it all came from God's
gracious initiative.

A promised seed

By the time we get to the birth of Isaac, the scale of the
promise has become clear. God will build a great nation
– more than that, God will bless the world through the
offspring of Abraham. Isaac, the promised seed, would
be the bearer of the covenant promises of God.

> I will establish my covenant with him as an
> everlasting covenant for his descendants after him.
> (Genesis 17:19)

At 100 years of age Abraham finally had the promised
son. Sarah, at ninety, had coped with the trauma of birth
and now at last the restoration of mankind's rebellion
in the garden appeared to be underway. Yet the chapter
after Isaac was born, Abraham is instructed to sacrifice
him. The text presents us with a cold and sober record
of what happened. 'Early the next morning Abraham

got up and saddled his donkey.' (Genesis 22:3). No ifs or buts, no protestations. Abraham did what God had told him.

Isaac followed his father, trusting his every decision, not knowing what lay ahead. As they approached the place of sacrifice, carrying the wood for the fire, he asked, 'where is the lamb for the burnt offering?' (Genesis 22:7). Abraham replied 'God will provide.'

Did he really think that? Would God provide when God had just commanded him to sacrifice his own son? Perhaps Abraham was twisting the truth to cope with his own emotions and ease the path for the unsuspecting victim. Genesis doesn't tell us what Abraham thought. But the letter to the Hebrews in the New Testament does.

> By faith Abraham, when God tested him, offered Isaac as a sacrifice. He who had received the promises was about to sacrifice his one and only son, even though God had said to him, 'it is through Isaac that your offspring will be reckoned.' Abraham reasoned that God could raise the dead, and figuratively speaking, he did receive Isaac back from death (Hebrews 11:17-19).

Abraham knew what it meant to trust God. If God could produce a child from a ninety-year-old barren woman, he could raise a boy from the dead. Abraham was not lying to Isaac, he was putting his trust in a God who had proved himself trustworthy. God would provide – and in his mercy and grace he did. For at the moment of sacrifice an angel appeared, acknowledging the faith of Abraham and providing a ram, a substitute sacrifice, to be offered to God.

A better son

A promised people, a promised land, a promised seed.
Everything was in place for a restoration of Eden – God's
people once again enjoying God's blessing. And yet Eden
wasn't restored and Satan (the serpent) was not crushed
(as had been promised in Genesis 3). Yes, God had
graciously intervened in history and made wonderful
promises, guaranteed with his own life. But the Old
Testament does not stop there. The people rebel, the
land is destroyed and the offspring falter. So if the
promises stand, how are they to be fulfilled?

The promised nation

The New Testament opens to the politically turbulent
world of the first century. The chequered history of the
descendants of Abraham conspired to fuel the religious
and national fervour of the Jews in their now occupied
country. They could not forget the promise to their
'fathers,' Abraham, Isaac and Jacob. They were still
looking for a great nation and great blessing in a land of
their own. But the words of the New Testament came
as a shock to many whose ultimate hope had not been
placed in the one to whom all the promises pointed.
Even before the ministry of Jesus began, John the Baptist
challenged them with these words:

> Do not begin to say to yourselves, 'We have
> Abraham as our father.' For I tell you that out of
> these stones God can raise up children for Abraham.
> (Luke 3:8)

Clearly, simple descent was not the answer. The identity
of the promised nation lay elsewhere. According to the

New Testament the identity of the people of God is not defined by genetics but by Jesus:

> Understand, then, that those who believe are children of Abraham. The Scripture foresaw that God would justify the Gentiles by faith, and announced the gospel in advance to Abraham: 'All nations will be blessed through you.' So those who have faith are blessed along with Abraham, the man of faith . . . Jesus redeemed us in order that the blessing given to Abraham might come to the Gentiles through Christ Jesus, so that by faith we might receive the promise of the Spirit. (Galatians 3:7-9, 14)

As God took the elderly, childless and nomadic Abram out of his tent and made him look up at the stars, the descendants of which he spoke were those who would trust the promises of God fulfilled in Christ. You and I, if we believe, are children of Abraham, part of God's nation. One day we will see and experience the promise to Abraham in all its fullness as together with all who have trusted Christ, we will be part of 'a great multitude that no-one could count, from every nation, tribe, people and language, standing before the throne and in front of the lamb.' (Revelation 7:9)

The promised land

The collateral for God's promise of land was his own death. When Abram fell into a deep sleep, it was God, not Abram, who passed through the pieces of the covenant sacrifice to guarantee his promise. Come what may, God's people would have a land of their own. But as we have seen God's people are not simply those who have descended physically from Abraham – and in the same way God's promised land is not simply the geographical region that continues to be the breeding ground for tension and war. In the Old Testament it was divided, attacked and occupied. When Jesus was born it was under Roman rule. When Jesus died the promise was finally secured and the land guaranteed – not a land bound by politics and geography but a land defined by God and accessed through faith in Jesus.

> For Abraham was looking forward to the city with foundations, whose architect and builder is God. [Abraham and his family] were looking for a better country – a heavenly one. Therefore God is not ashamed to be called their God, for he has prepared a city for them.   (Hebrews 11:10,16)

The promised land is that which we read about at the end of the Bible and we will see at the end of time . . .

> Then I saw a new heaven and a new earth, for the first heaven and the first earth had passed away . . . and I saw the Holy City, the New Jerusalem, coming out of heaven from God, prepared as a bride beautifully dressed for her husband. And I heard a loud voice from the throne saying 'Now the dwelling of God is with men, and he will live with them. They will be his people, and God himself will be with them and be their God.' (Revelation 21:1-3)

God promised the land to Abraham *on* pain of death and he secured the land through Jesus *in* the pain of death.

The promised seed

Matthew begins his gospel with some striking words. 'A record of the genealogy of Jesus Christ, the son of David, the son of Abraham.' (Matthew 1:1). The real seed of Abraham to whom all the promises pointed was not Isaac, or Jacob, but Jesus. He was and is the one through whom we become part of the promised nation and receive the promised land. The blessings promised to Abraham and his descendants are the blessings received in Christ – the one who carried his cross to be our sacrifice. This time no ram was found caught in the thicket – for unlike Abraham, God 'did not spare his own son, but gave him up for us all.' (Romans 8:32). At Calvary there was no substitute for Jesus. Rather, Jesus was a substitute for us.

So we have come from Adam to Abraham. The promise has been made. God will act. But it was to be many hundreds of years before the one to whom the promises pointed was born – years of conflict and tension, but years shaped by a faithful God – the God of Abraham and Isaac and Jacob.

NOTES:

[1] Gordon Wenham, Word Biblical Commentary Volume 1 *Genesis 1-15*, (Word,1987) p.li

[2] Graeme Goldsworthy *Gospel and Kingdom*, (Paternoster,1981) p.59

3

A Better Passover

Reuben looked at the little lamb that had been selected from the flock the day before. As far as he could see it was a perfect year-old male. Unlike the flocks and herds that had been part and parcel of his life in Egypt, this lamb was different. Reuben didn't play with him in the way he and the other children played with the sheep and goats that wandered amongst the sparse accommodation imposed by the Egyptian regime. Both Reuben and his parents knew only too well the instruction that God had given to the people through his servant Moses. This lamb was to be slaughtered and its blood was to be collected in a bowl before being painted over the lintel and doorframe of their humble house. But there was still anticipation and a certain nervousness as Reuben stroked the innocent victim.

'Father,' he said 'tell me again why we have to kill the lamb and paint his blood on the door posts.'
His father bent down and looked Reuben in the eye. 'Moses has told us that God will pass over Egypt on the fourteenth day of the month and he will strike down every firstborn – both men and animals – and will bring judgement on the gods of Egypt.'

The colour drained from Reuben's face. 'Father, I am your first born. It is three days to go until the fourteenth day of the month. Are you sure that I will not die too?'

37

'My son,' his father replied, 'You shall not die, you need have no fear, for this lamb will die in your place. Its blood will protect our household. We shall be free once again, free to go to the land God promised to our father Abraham.'

Hundreds of years had passed since God made the promise of land to Abraham. Famine and misfortune had brought Jacob (Isaac's son) and his large family to Egypt and through the sovereignty of God, Joseph (Jacob's son) had been raised up to secure the nation and settle the family in prosperity. The great dynasty was growing in the comfort of another land. But as the years passed 'a new king, who did not know about Joseph, came to power in Egypt.' (Exodus 1:8). He put slave-masters over the people of God to oppress them with forced labour. He treated them ruthlessly and sought to kill all male babies born to the Israelites. His regime was one of oppression, hatred and violence. Forced labour and genocide were the daily companions of God's chosen people.

It must have been frightening and confusing. God had promised a great land, a great nation and great blessing – but here they were, away from the land and in slavery to a foreign power. In the midst of their despair they cried out to the God of their fathers, the God of Abraham, Isaac and Jacob – and in hearing their cry, God called Moses to be their leader and their rescuer.

In many ways he was an unlikely candidate. Moses was no super-hero but an elderly ex-murderer who had been on the run. Undoubtedly he had a great sense of justice – his reason for fleeing was that he had killed an Egyptian for ill-treating one of his compatriots – but at the same he did not have much courage. Excuse after excuse followed his call – 'I'm a nobody, why should I go? What if they don't believe me? I'm not much of a public speaker. They won't listen to me.' But God would have none of it. He had heard the cries of his people, remembered his promise to Abraham and decided to rescue them. Moses was to be his rescuer, God-commissioned with the task of leading the people to freedom. And so it was that Moses' 'birth [was] the turning point towards an unseen, better future.'[1]

God would rescue his people. An event was about to happen that would shape the future of the people of Israel and find its fulfilment in the death of Jesus on the cross. It was an event surrounded by miracles and centred on the sacrifice of a lamb – the substitute that would bring freedom. That event was the Passover.

Miracles

When we compare the twenty-first century to the first century it is clear that miraculous events – healings and exorcisms – are far less frequent. God in his mercy does at times intervene to heal and restore but the overwhelming number and nature of miracles that we see associated with the ministry of Jesus when on earth have not been matched since the early days of the church. Some may say that it is because we lack faith, that our vision of God is too small, but a wider view of the Bible might make us think otherwise, and perhaps reassure us. The apostle Paul was not healed of his 'Thorn in the flesh' (2 Corinthians 12:7-9); he preached the gospel in Galatia because of an illness (Galatians 4:13,14), and at the end of his life as he outlined the essentials of ministry to the younger Timothy it was all about preaching the message of Jesus and the apostles – a message which had been accredited by miracles[2] but thereafter was not dependent on them.

Both the Old Testament and the New Testament reveal an intensity of the miraculous around two 'salvific events' (events involved with the salvation or rescue of God's people). The New Testament cluster of miracles is found around the ministry of Jesus and his apostles and the Old Testament cluster is found around the Passover and the rescue of the people from Egypt.

Both events were turning points in the history of God's dealings with the world. The Passover was an act of salvation or redemption in which the people of God were freed from his wrath by the blood of a lamb so that they might enjoy the freedom of his presence and the promise of his blessing. So was the death of Jesus. He had come to take away the sin of the world – to die on a cross so that those who trust him could be rescued *from* his wrath and redeemed *for* the freedom of his presence in heaven. And just as the Old Testament looks back to the miraculous events of the Passover and the Exodus that followed it, so the New Testament sees the miracles which surround the ministry of Jesus as authenticating factors in accrediting both his identity and his mission.

The Old Testament, the Passover and the Exodus

The Old Testament encouraged God's people to look back to these events in order to teach the next generation of God's gracious salvation:

> He did miracles in the sight of their fathers in the land of Egypt, in the region of Zoan. He divided the sea and led them through; he made the water stand firm like a wall. He guided them with the cloud by day and with light from the fire all night. He split

the rocks in the desert and gave them water as
abundant as the seas; he brought streams out of a
rocky crag and made water flow down like rivers.
(Psalm 78:12-16)

The Psalm tells us that the epoch-making events of the
Passover and the Exodus were surrounded by a cluster
of miracles which gave them divine credibility. God had
rescued the people – miraculously.

The New Testament and the death of Jesus

Jesus was God's ultimate salvation, to which the Passover
and the events of the Old Testament pointed. And as
with the Passover and Exodus, the 'salvific' events
associated with Jesus were authenticated by the
miraculous:

Jesus of Nazareth was a man accredited by God to
you by miracles, wonders and signs, which God did
among you through him. (Acts 2:22)

Once again, signs, wonders and miracles point us to
God's activity in history. God has done something in
Christ so that we might come to know him, free from
the condemnation of sin and certain of our future in
heaven. God still intervenes in the world and by his grace
he still intervenes miraculously (not least in people
coming to faith), but we shouldn't expect as many
miracles in the twenty-first century as we read of in the
first – because the ministry of Jesus has been
authenticated. The lamb has been slain. The people are
free.

Substitution

In the Old Testament, Israel is described as God's first-born son, the inheritor of his promises. It was therefore all the more significant (and dangerous), that Pharaoh would not free Israel from slavery. Pharaoh was unknowingly playing with a greater king than himself and was thereby inviting the judgement of God. If 'Pharaoh would not release God's firstborn, then God's judgement would fall on Pharaoh's firstborn and on the oldest son in every Egyptian household.'[3]

God's judgement was to be just and universal. There would be no difference – death would result in every household, both Israelite and Egyptian. The difference was that in the Israelite households God would provide a substitute. A lamb would die instead of a son. Its blood would be shed in the place of another. As such there would be 'equivalence' or justice.

Alec Motyer, in his excellent book, *Look to the Rock*, writes:

> The remarkable strong emphasis on the element of equivalence in the choice of the lamb (Exodus 12:3-5) coupled with the reality of a death in every house (12:30) and the balance between the firstborn of Pharaoh and Israel as the corporate firstborn of the Lord (4:22) are, without question, best summed up by saying that the Passover lamb was a substitute.[4]

In the same way, Jesus was our substitute, our 'Passover Lamb' (1 Corinthians 5:7). As he celebrated his final Passover, just before his death, his words and his actions made the connection clear. Every year Jews celebrated the day when the lamb died in their place so that their forefathers could be free. By the time Jesus entered public life that freedom and the hope of the promised land which it brought were yet again a political and religious concern. The Romans occupied the land. The people wanted to be free again and religious fervour was high as Jerusalem's population swelled threefold for the Passover celebrations.

Jesus died at the time of the Passover, with all the imagery and history of the Passover brought sharply into focus. Three years earlier as Jesus began his public ministry, John the Baptist had identified Jesus as 'The lamb of God who takes away the sin of the world,' (John 1:29) and now on the cross the association ran even deeper. Jesus was the perfect firstborn son, Jesus took the judgement of God in his death (represented by the darkness in the middle of the day) and Jesus died without his legs being broken, just as had been instructed for the Passover lamb:

> Because the Jews did not want the bodies left on the crosses during the Sabbath, they asked Pilate to have the legs broken and the bodies taken down. The soldiers therefore came and broke the legs of the first man who had been crucified with Jesus, and then those of the other. But when they came to Jesus and found that he was already dead, they did not break his legs. Instead, one of the soldiers pierced Jesus' side with a spear, bringing a sudden flow of blood and water . . . these things happened so that scripture would be fulfilled: 'Not one of his bones will be broken.' (John 19:31-34, 36)

There is of course one major difference between the Passover lamb of Egypt and Jesus as the 'new' Passover lamb: whereas God the king 'provided' the lamb in the Old Testament, it was God the king who *was* the lamb in the New – for the word that became flesh was none other than the lamb of God who takes away the sin of the world.

Freedom

The Passover brought freedom. The people were no longer under the tyrannical rule of Pharaoh. They were free to serve their God and travel to the land he had promised to Abraham all those years before. This was a freedom to be God's people, enslaved to him rather than a foreign dictator. It was not therefore what many today perceive as freedom. When we talk about liberty we often mean that lack of constraints and confinement which enable us to do what we want. We want to be free to serve ourselves, not God.

The freedom of the Passover did not entertain such liberty. It brought freedom *from* the tyranny of one king and rescued the people *for* the service of another – that of their creator God. And so 'Passover night redefined Israel's problem. Hitherto they had lived under the threat of a genocidal king, but now a new factor came into being. Another king is on his way, even more feared and inescapable than Pharaoh.'[5]

The Passover was therefore about both deliverance and redemption. The people had been released from slavery and redeemed, or bought back, by God for his service. They had been released, but they still had a responsibility to live as God's freed people, in the renewed relationship secured by the Passover. Freedom from the land of Egypt might have changed the address of God's people but 'A change of address is not a change of heart nor is the dissolution of an old bondage to Pharaoh the initiation of a new relationship with the

Lord, there are two sides to the Exodus work – 'out of Egypt' and 'to myself.'"[6]

When we turn our attention to the New Testament and the Lord Jesus Christ, to whom the Passover and events of the Exodus point, we see a similar deliverance and redemption. Through his sacrificial death, his blood shed for us, we too are delivered from the slavery of sin and protected from the judgement of God – but it is not a freedom *for* sin but a freedom *from* sin. His death enables us to be redeemed, bought back, so that we might serve our creator. That is true freedom. That is true Christianity.

In my experience people love the idea of forgiveness. It enables the slate to be wiped clean, the guilt to be removed and a new start to be made. But the Christian gospel is about repentance – turning around. Jesus' death enables me to turn around because the barrier of my sin has been removed – and once that sin has been removed I am free to serve the Lord, adopted into God's family as his child. That is the freedom of being a slave of Christ. As a friend of mine often says – if you have not been told that you are always a slave, either to Christ or to sin, you have not been told the gospel.

NOTES:
[1] John Durham Word Biblical Commentary Volume 3, *Exodus* (Word,1987) p.17
[2] See Acts 2:22
[3] Edmund Clowney *The Unfolding Mystery*, (Navipress,1988) p.90
[4] Alec Motyer *Look to the Rock* IVP 1996 p.53
[5] ibid. p.49
[6] ibid. p.48

4

A Better Covenant

Will you love her, comfort her, honour and protect
her, and, forsaking all others, be faithful to her as
long as you both shall live?[1]

It is a real privilege to have a job which involves taking
weddings. They are times of such happiness, fun and
laughter. At the same time it is a real responsibility.
When an engaged couple visit the clergyman who will
be taking their wedding it is the first meeting they will
have in the process of preparation that will be concerned
more about the marriage than the wedding day. Cakes,
flowers, photographs and food aside, the questions asked
by the officiating clergyman are profound. They take
the focus off the wedding dress and onto lifelong
commitment.

Sometimes it has been at that meeting when concerns
have crept in – I remember one couple who had been
living together for several years. They had decided to
get married because the relationship 'was going
nowhere.' 'And what about the promise of life-long
commitment you will make?', I asked. 'If it works, it
works. If it doesn't, it doesn't,' came the reply. There
was little or no awareness that a promise is a promise –
that certain commitments are non-negotiable.

The reason I start here in this chapter on covenant is because we live in a society where the notion of committed agreement between two parties is poorly understood. Yes, we make commitments, but for many they mean little. A marriage brings physical union and often financial union. It brings legal and public commitment in the form of binding documents and rings. It contains a public declaration of promises made in the name of God. Yet statistics reveal that all such 'promises' can amount to little. Even the most profound and personal 'covenant,' that of marriage, is losing its currency.

When our thoughts turn to God and his 'promise' or 'covenant' such opting out is simply inconceivable. The Biblical word which we translate as covenant denotes 'an irrevocable decision which cannot be cancelled by anyone.'[2] So as we come to think about covenant we do so with the absolute certainty that the covenant initiated by God is a covenant that cannot and will not be broken.

The Strength of the Covenant

Cast your mind back to Abram. God made a covenant with him and sealed it with sacrifice and blood. He had taken the initiative to remedy mankind's problem.

> So the Lord said to him, 'Bring me a heifer, a goat and a ram, each three years old, along with a dove and a young pigeon.
>
> Abram brought all these to him, cut them in two and arranged the halves opposite each other . . . when the sun had set and darkness had fallen, a smoking brazier with a blazing torch appeared and passed between the pieces. On that day the LORD made a

covenant with Abram and said, 'To your descendants
I give this land. (Genesis 15: 9,10,17,18)

So often when we make a promise we either don't want
to carry it out (if the initiative has come from us) or else
we are impotent to do anything about it (if the initiative
has come from someone else). A few years ago a friend
of the family promised my son a ride in his vintage car.
My son never forgot the promise and every time he saw
the car he hoped that the promise would be fulfilled –
but he was powerless to do anything about it. Only the
one who made the promise could act. After three years
of uncertainty the promised ride finally materialised.
Now it is not the promise but the fulfilment of the
promise which is remembered.

The people of God had to wait far longer for their
promise to be fulfilled – but because it was God who
made the promise, there could be absolute certainty that
it would be remembered. His character secured his word.

God heard their groaning and he remembered his
covenant with Abraham, with Isaac and with Jacob.
So God looked on the Israelites and was concerned
about them (Exodus 2:24,25).

The Passover and the Exodus were a direct consequence
of God's initiative. God's character and faithfulness
prompted him to act. He rescued the people for himself
because he had made an unshakeable promise to
Abraham. The day the Israelites left Egypt they were
free, liberated to serve their creator, covenant God. He
would take them into the desert to confirm and deepen
that very covenant relationship which had begun all
those years before with Abram. The desert wanderings

had a direction – as the people journeyed into the wilderness their destination was to be Mount Sinai.

> And God said 'I will be with you. And this will be the sign to you that it is I who have sent you: When you have brought the people out of Egypt, you will worship God on this mountain.' (Exodus 3:12)

God would take the people to Sinai. Thus the promise to an individual (Abraham) *for* a nation was to develop into a promise through an individual (Moses) *with* a nation. At Sinai those who knew they were God's people by the promise to Abraham and their rescue from Egypt agreed to live in such a way that they would be recognised as God's people, his 'kingdom of priests and a holy nation' (Exodus 19:6), through whom God would bring his long-promised reconciliation to the world.

The Pattern of the Promise

When the people arrived at Mount Sinai they gathered before the mountain, shrouded in the fire and cloud of the unapproachable holiness of God. There he gave his people the law, confirming it with a covenantal sacrifice.

> When Moses went and told the people all the LORD's words and laws, they all responded with one voice, 'Everything the LORD has said we will do.' Moses then wrote down everything the LORD had said. He got up early the next morning and built an altar at the foot of the mountain and set up twelve stone pillars representing the twelve tribes of Israel. Then he sent young Israelite men, and they offered burnt offerings and sacrificed young bulls as fellowship offerings to the LORD. Moses took half of the blood and put it in bowls, and the other half he sprinkled

on the altar. Then he took the Book of the Covenant and read it to all the people. They responded, 'We will do everything the Lord has said; We will obey.' Moses then took the blood, sprinkled it on the people and said, 'This is the blood of the covenant that the Lord has made with you in accordance with all these words." (Exodus 24:3-8)

The covenant with Abraham laid the foundation on which the Covenant with the people at Sinai (what we might call the 'Mosaic Covenant') was built. In Genesis God had promised to make a people and provide a land. Here in the book of Exodus God was instructing those promised people how to live as his people. The 'law' was therefore the God given pattern for holy living. It was the way in which those who had been rescued and redeemed to *be* God's people could be distinguished *as* God's people. The law was the 'divinely given pattern of life which God sets before and upon a redeemed people.'[3]

But no sooner had the law been given than it was broken. The first of the Ten Commandments was 'You shall have no other gods before me' (Exodus 20:3). The people had heard the conditions of the Book of the Covenant and had agreed to keep it. To a man they had shouted, 'we will do it.' And no-one there could have failed to realize the implication of not keeping the law – the image of the covenantal ceremony would not allow it. Bull's blood dripped from the altar at the foot of the mountain; its metallic sweetness permeated the air as it clung to the clothing and hair of those on whom it had been sprinkled. They knew that the consequence of breaking the covenant would be death – in the same way that a bull died to seal the covenant, they would die if they broke it.

Moses had only been up the mountain for forty days and forty nights when it all went wrong. The covenant ceremony was still fresh in the minds of those who had agreed to keep the law – but their hearts were elsewhere. In the absence of their leader the people decided to 'make gods' to go before them. They were consciously breaking the covenant – and with it they were heaping upon themselves the curses which were a part of that very law they had agreed to keep:

> If you reject my decrees and abhor my laws and fail to carry out all my commands and so violate my covenant, then I will do this to you . . . I myself will be hostile towards you and will afflict you for your sins seven times over. And I will bring the sword upon you to avenge the breaking of the covenant. (Leviticus 26:15,16,24-25)

Here was a covenant keeping God with a covenant breaking people – a people who knew of his rescue and redemption from bondage in Egypt and a people who knew the consequence of breaking the covenant they had promised to keep. Disobedience would bring death. The people who had been rescued and who had praised God with their lips, promising to live in obedience to his law, had found that their hearts were unable to match their mouths. It is often said that the heart of the human problem is the problem of the human heart. Such was their problem – and such is ours. How many times have we known what is right and chosen what is wrong? How many times have we found ourselves irresistibly drawn to sin when we know that its consequences would bring ruin? How often have we praised God with our lips on a Sunday morning only to curse him and others with those same lips on a Monday morning? How often have we used the hands we lift in prayer to fuel and express our sinful desires? We may hear God's law and say with the Israelites 'we will do it' but we cannot – our hearts have failed. And if 'the point of failure which prompts the onset of the curses of the covenant is the failure of the heart of man, the uncircumcised heart [then] that is where the remedy needs to be applied.'[4]

The Fulfilment of the Promise

The Covenant at Sinai leaves us with a picture of a covenant-keeping God and a covenant-breaking people – a people who need a new heart if they are to be obedient but who deserve to die for their disobedience. God's holiness and justice demand that the consequence of covenantal disobedience be met, but God's love for those who are disobedient drives him yet again to take the initiative with his wayward creation so that they can be reconciled to him. God promises a new heart and with it, a new life.

A new heart

As the years rolled by, the disobedience of a covenant-breaking people continued. It resulted in internal division, occupation of the promised land and eventually destruction, culminating in Jerusalem, God's holy city, being razed to the ground and the temple, God's symbolic dwelling place, lying in ruins. The people of God, rescued by him from Egyptian slavery, had forgotten their past and forfeited their future in selfish disobedience. As a result they experienced all that God had promised to those who fail to keep the covenant agreed by their forefathers at the foot of the mountain all those years before.

It was at the height of this devastation, in the sixth Century BC as the consequence of disobedience was reaching its zenith, that through the prophet Jeremiah God promised something new.

> 'The time is coming,' declares the LORD, 'when I will make a new covenant with the house of Israel and with the house of Judah. It will not be like the covenant I made with their forefathers when I took them by the hand to lead them out of Egypt, because they broke my covenant, though I was a husband to them,' declares the LORD. 'This is the covenant that I will make with the house of Israel after that time,' declares the LORD. 'I will put my law in their minds and write it on their hearts. I will be their God, and they will be my people.' (Jeremiah 31:31-33)

In making such a promise God was not setting aside all that had happened at Sinai. The binding nature of the contract still stood, the covenantal curses still remained. God had pledged himself to its conditions and consequences. The law remained the expected ethical outworking of those who had been rescued by the blood of the lamb. But in Jeremiah we see a more personal application of the grace of God that underlies all of God's dealing with humanity. The promise is that God, the divine physician, will not only supply the medicine of righteousness – telling us how to live as his people – but he will administer it himself, so that through his activity a new heart will be given, a heart willing and able to live as part of God's righteous people. The people may have rebelled, but God remained faithful and therefore he alone, 'as founder of the covenant, could guarantee its continuance . . . only he could renew the covenant broken by human disobedience.'[5]

Renewal of the covenant did not mean abandonment of its conditions. Death was still the consequence of disobedience and so death was still required if the covenant conditions were to be met and a new heart was to be attained. But it was to be God himself, in the Lord Jesus Christ, who died on behalf of and in the place of his rebellious people. God had set the standards for his redeemed people and in Christ's death he met those standards. And so 'The blood of Jesus as the covenant-mediator establishes and implements the divine promises.'[6]

A new life

When Jesus ate his last Passover meal with the disciples they were doing far more than remembering the freedom from Egypt all those years before. As Jesus took the bread and gave it to his disciples the words he spoke refocused their thoughts. No longer were they to remember the affliction of their Jewish forefathers and their release from Pharaoh's vindictive rule. Now they were to remember him. Jesus was now the 'Passover lamb' who was about to die to take away the sins of the world.

After supper he took the cup – much as any Jew would do in the Passover celebrations – but this time Jesus added the words, 'This is my blood of the covenant' (or new covenant)[7]. In saying those words Jesus was bringing together the Passover, the covenant at Sinai and Jeremiah's promise of a new covenant – all was to be focused on him and fulfilled in him. In his death Jesus was the new Passover lamb; in his death he fulfilled the people's side of the agreement at Sinai and in his death he took the punishment for sin, thereby applying God's remedy, his medication, so that it could become possible to have the promised new heart. Jesus fulfilled the righteous requirements of the law in his death. He died instead of the people. God had both set the standards and met the standards in the Lord Jesus Christ.

So it was that the covenant-keeping God restored the covenant-breaking people by becoming one of them. Yet unlike them, Jesus was perfect. Where they failed (and where we fail), Jesus succeeded – and what we deserve Jesus takes – for he died the death of others; not only to win their freedom but also to deal with their disobedience. In his death he was both the Passover lamb and the covenant fulfiller.

It is therefore possible through faith in Christ to have the promised new heart and to enjoy a promised new life, free from the slavery of sin and the tyranny of death. The punishment has been taken, the covenant has been fulfilled and perfected. This new covenant, sealed with Jesus' own blood is 'better in assured hope (Hebrews 7:22-25) – in that he is endlessly alive to administer its benefits; better in promises (Hebrews 8:6), for sins will be remembered no more; resting on a better sacrifice (Hebrews 9:13-14, 23-28), the once for all death of Jesus (Hebrews 9:28; 10:12).'[8]

We started with a picture of marriage. It is a picture found in the Old Testament and New Testament to explain the nature of God's commitment to us. The people may have been faithless but God is unshakeably faithful. His promise is not 'till death us do part' but 'because of my death we will never part.' That is a better covenant.

NOTES:

[1] ASB Marriage Service, The Central Board of Finance of the Church of England 1980

[2] *The Dictionary of New Testament Theology,* Volume 1, (Paternoster Press Revised Edition,1986) p.365

[3] *Old Testament Covenant Theology* (lectures 1973/1974) UCCF p.17

[4] Alec Motyer, *Look to the Rock* (IVP, 1996) p.23

[5] *The Dictionary of New Testament Theology* Volume 1 (Paternoster Press Revised Edition,1986) p.367

[6] Motyer, p.61

[7] Paul and Luke include the word 'New.'

[8] Motyer, p.61

5

A Better Law

The place of the law in the Bible has provoked a wealth of literature and debate. Many people assume that the Old Testament has a 'gospel' of salvation by works whilst the New Testament has a 'gospel' of grace. Others try and keep the ten commandments, but are less concerned or aware of the verses in the chapters that follow, which include such instructions as 'Anyone who curses his father or mother must be put to death.' (Exodus 21:17). When we read of the 'law' in the New Testament it seems to be spoken of in a negative way – the 'letter' killing (2 Corinthians 3:6)[1] – and when we read of it in the Old Testament it seems too difficult to keep. We are left asking 'Why have the law? What is its purpose? And what is its relevance today?'

We might be further confused by the heading of this chapter – ' A better law' – which would suggest the old one was no good and a new one, presumably instituted by Jesus, is better. But then we read what Jesus said:

'Do not think that I have come to abolish the Law or the Prophets: I have not come to abolish them but to fulfil them. I tell you the truth, until heaven and earth disappear, not the smallest letter, not the least stroke of a pen, will by any means disappear from the Law until everything is accomplished.' (Matthew 5:17,18)

. . . And what Paul said:

> So then, the law is holy, and the commandment is holy, righteous and good. (Romans 7:12)

It all appears very confusing – especially when the Bible has so much to say about how God's people are to live. We need to go back to the Old Testament and continue our story a little further before seeing how Jesus and the New Testament make sense of this apparently perplexing problem.

The law before Christ

A people formed by the law

God has always instructed his people how to live. Way back in the Garden of Eden God gave a 'law' in that he told Adam and Eve not to eat the fruit from the tree of the knowledge of good and evil. Such a command was not restrictive but liberating. If kept, it allowed total freedom within the garden and in relationship to God. If broken, all freedom would be removed and death would result. In that sense law was 'both the guardian and guarantor of liberty.'[2]

Hundreds of years later, after God had promised restoration through the covenant with Abraham and had rescued his people from slavery in Egypt, he then once again gave law to the people – people who heard his words and gladly agreed to accept their responsibility in keeping his commands. Contrary to much popular thought, 'the giving of the law [at Sinai] was not a new bondage but a charter for the free, a token that slavery and bondage [was] over.'[3]

God's programme of salvation was therefore always by grace. His promise to Abraham came from a divine initiative to a rebellious people. The God who had made such promises and had rescued the people from their slavery to the Egyptians was not then enslaving them with higher demands before bringing them to the land he had previously promised unconditionally. This was no mid-desert programme of salvation by works, but a God-given pattern of living for God's holy people – a people who had been rescued by God's gracious initiative and were now being corporately marked out as God's people so that they could be a 'holy nation and a royal priesthood.' (Exodus 19:6).

But the standards were high – perhaps we might say impossibly so. The civil, moral and ceremonial injunctions covered all aspects of life. There was no escape for those who held the label of 'God's treasured possession.'(Exodus 19:5). The reason for such high standards of holiness in God's people was that God himself was so holy. Their behaviour was to reflect his character; by obeying the Law they would become like him:

> The LORD said to Moses, 'Speak to the entire assembly of Israel and say to them: "Be holy because I, the LORD your God, am holy."' (Leviticus 19:1-2)

A people failed by the law

The problem was that the people did not keep the law. Their wholehearted acceptance and affirmation of the covenantal consequences of being God's people soon wore off with the delay in Moses' return from the mountain. Again and again we see that the commands they were given were commands which they couldn't – and often wouldn't – keep.

By the time the people were established in their own land with a flourishing temple and an elaborate system of sacrifices, the hearts of many were far away from the redeeming love shown to their forefathers as they were rescued from Egypt. In their minds the law was still important, but it had become thought of in terms of the visible mark of membership of God's people, rather than as a response to the saving grace of the Passover and Exodus. Their attempted legalistic obedience to the law became to them the distinguishing mark between Jew and non-Jew.

The law itself had not changed. It was still good and God-given. It remained the expected outworking of those who had experienced the loving rescue of God – but the hearts of those seeking to apply it had hardened. Outwardly they were often rigorous in their application (and interpretation) of the law and their attempt to live it. They wanted a form of righteousness and ethnic distinction that law observance might bring. And yet it was impossible – the law was never designed to achieve righteousness and can therefore never produce righteousness (a right standing before God)[4].

If they were to live as God lived and be the people he wanted them to be, they needed a new heart – the new heart promised by God through the prophet Jeremiah – and they needed to recognize that without God's grace, his standards would always be too holy for mortal man to attain. Once again, sin was the problem that prevented God's people truly living as God's people; and 'law cannot overcome sin because it depends on the co-operation of the flesh, which is weak.'[5] Israel would not obey the law. Israel could not obey the law. They needed a new heart – a heart that only Christ can provide.

The law after Christ

We are still left asking why the law was given. It is all
very well to say that obedience to the law was the
expected outworking of God's redeemed people, but
God's redeemed people could not do it. Sin had
weakened their ability to live as God's treasured
possession. It is only when we turn to the pages of the
New Testament that we see the bigger picture and begin
to understand why the law was there and how it might
be relevant for us today. According to the New
Testament the Law draws us to Jesus by acting as a
prison, a servant and a prophet.

The law as prison

In his letter to the churches in Galatia, the apostle Paul
wrote:

> . . . if a law had been given that could impart life,
> then righteousness would certainly have come by
> the law. But the scripture declares that the whole
> world is a prisoner of sin. . . (Galatians 3:21, 22a)

The picture here is of a jail sentence with scripture as
the magistrate, mankind as the prisoner and 'sin as the
jailer who carries out the sentence.'[6]

Scripture declares the whole world to be sinners in
that it 'locks up all men' under the condemnation of sin
such that there is no possibility of escape. It does this so
that 'What was promised, being given through faith in
Jesus Christ, might be given to those who believe.'
(Galatians 3:22b)

The law therefore holds mankind prisoner, shut up
by his sin and unable to break free and secure his right
standing before God in any other way than by holding

to the promise given to Abraham – the promise manifested in the rescue from Egypt and fully revealed in the Lord Jesus Christ, to whom the law points and in whom it is fulfilled.

The *law as servant*

As we move a little further in the letter to the Galatians, Paul describes the law as the *paidagogos*, the one whose responsibility it is to 'lead us to Christ,' as the New International Version records it (Galatians 3:24). In ancient society the *paidagogos* (literally 'boy-leader') was the servant or slave who had the responsibility of overseeing the conduct of the wealthy freeborn children until those children reached their maturity. Although he was a slave and therefore under the master of the family, he had authority over the master's children.

The term does not suggest that the law had an educative role. It did not make those to whom it was given increasingly aware of their need for God. Rather, Paul means that the law held people and in some senses kept them until the revelation of Christ, when its responsibility ceased. In that way, one role of the law (as *paidagogos*) was fulfilled when Jesus came – the law became obsolete, part of the old dispensation. Its custodianship was over. The child had reached maturity.

But a hasty abandonment of the law would be to throw the baby out with the bath water and would not do justice to scripture. We must turn to our third metaphor, employed by Jesus himself, if we are to complete our picture.

The law as prophet

Jesus had much to say about the role of the law in relation to his own mission and ministry. Two particular references are pertinent to our discussion:

> Do not think that I have come to abolish the Law or the Prophets; I have not come to abolish them but to fulfil them. (Matthew 5:17)

> For all the Prophets and the Law prophesied until John. (Matthew 11:13)

It is clear from these verses that 'the law itself has some kind of forward-looking element.'[7] It wasn't an end in itself, but found its end in Christ[8]. It must therefore be in our understanding of Christ that we find both the fulfilment of the law and its continuing relevance for Christians today. For while Jesus never suggests that he or his followers are free to disobey or abandon the Old Testament scriptures, his teaching and his actions do give us some understanding of how the law is to be viewed and applied.

In his commentary on these verses, D.A. Carson helpfully sums up how the law related to Christ and his followers:

> The law pointed forward to Jesus and his teaching, so it is properly obeyed by conforming to his word. As it points to him, so he, in fulfilling it, established what continuity it has, the true direction to which it points and the way it is to be obeyed . . . his teaching, towards which the Old Testament points, must be obeyed.[9]

And so it is in Christ and his teaching that we find the key to the law. It is to him we must now turn.

The law in the Christian life

The Sermon on the Mount (Matthew 5-7) provides sobering reading. Far from being a simple manifesto for human living – as it so often seems to be taken – it is a profound declaration of kingdom standards, the standards expected by Jesus of those who follow him. Jesus teaches that the righteousness of the Christian is to surpass the highest known standards of Jesus' day – that of the Pharisees.

> For I tell you that unless your righteousness surpasses that of the Pharisees and the teachers of the law, you will certainly not enter the kingdom of heaven. (Matthew 5:20)

These are strong words. They mean that the standard of Jesus 'Far from being lenient, is nothing more than perfection.'[10]

The Sermon on the Mount forces us to our knees as we cry out 'I cannot do it; it is too difficult for me!' We cannot but admit our utter inability to live by the standards of the king. Our sin has crippled our ability to obey – and so there is nowhere else to go for mercy but to the king who set the standards. His words drive us to his cross, for there, in his death, he secured what we could never do.

> For what the law was powerless to do in that it was weakened by the sinful nature, God did by sending his own Son in the likeness of sinful man to be a sin offering. And so he condemned sin in sinful man, in order that the righteous requirements of the law might be fully met in us. (Romans 8:3,4a)

The cross forces us to accept two realities about the law. The first is its importance. As Christians we cannot say that the Old Testament law is irrelevant. On the contrary 'The law obedience of the people of God is so important to God that he sent his son to die for us and his spirit to live in us in order to secure it.'[11] How we live is therefore of huge importance to God. His grace does not drive us away from right behaviour but drives us towards it.

Secondly the cross tells us that in and of ourselves we are powerless to live lives of obedience. We require forgiveness and the new life of the Spirit if we are to have any hope or desire of living by kingdom standards. Only then can God empower us to obey the law, not in a self-righteous perfectionism but in a Spirit-secured obedience. As Christians we will therefore delight in the teaching of Jesus, despair at our weakness in keeping it and be driven to the cross for forgiveness and to our knees in dependence on the Spirit for help. For 'Only the Spirit can take those dead in trespasses and sins and make them alive. And once one is made alive, he is able to respond positively and affectionately to the law for the first time.'[12]

The law of Christ

Jesus' own teaching and that of his commissioned disciples helps us to understand how we might live – and how we might obey the law – in our own day and age. Having said that the law points to him, Jesus then teaches what it means for the Christian to live the law:

> So in everything, do to others what you would have them do to you, for this sums up the Law and the Prophets. (Matthew 7:12)

Jesus replied 'Love the Lord your God with all your heart and with all your soul and with all you mind.' This is the first and greatest commandment. And the second is like it: 'Love your neighbour as yourself.' All the Law and the Prophets hang on these two commandments. (Matthew 22:37-40)

Likewise, Jesus' commissioned apostles teach about 'law':

Love does no harm to its neighbour. Therefore love is the fulfilment of the law. (Romans 13:10)

Carry each other's burdens, and in this way you will fulfil the law of Christ. (Galatians 6:2)

If you really keep the royal law found in scripture 'Love you neighbour as yourself' you are doing right. (James 2:8)

In every case cited above, the outworking of 'law' (using the term in its New Testament sense), will be seen in how Christians relate to God and to those around them – the vertical and horizontal relationships, as I have written elsewhere.[13] The Christian's response to the gracious initiative of God is not in keeping certain community laws or religious laws of the Old Testament, but in loving one another as Jesus did. Therefore the validity of the Old Testament law is found in how it relates to Jesus and his teaching. Where he teaches us to uphold an Old Testament teaching, then we must do so. Where he fulfils it or supersedes it (as in with the temple and sacrificial system) we are to submit to it only so far as it points to Christ. It has served its purpose.

The law therefore 'remains a permanent and crucial revelation of the will of God, but its application can no longer be by the simple observance of all its precepts as literal regulations for Christian conduct. The key to its interpretation is in Jesus and in his teaching, with its sovereign declaration of the will of God at a far deeper level than mere rule-keeping.'[14]

Our tendency will always be to fall back into religious legalism at the expense of real relationships. Jesus teaches the opposite. It is the quality of our relationships and our love that will mark us out as his people – his treasured possession – and therefore as 'doers' of the law. Such love is not soapy or superficial, but serious and sacrificial. It is a love that should be prepared take us to our death for another – just as Jesus did for us.

NOTES:

[1] 'He has made us competent as ministers of a new covenant – not of the letter but of the Spirit; for the letter kills, but the Spirit gives life.' 2 Corinthians 3:6

[2] Alec Motyer *Look to the Rock* (IVP,1996) p.76

[3] Motyer p.76

[4] 'Mankind, belonging to this age and standing under the dominion of sin and the flesh, inevitably perverts [the commandments] into a means of meritorious achievement, of religious boasting before God, so that keeping the law becomes a sinful effort to be independent of God and his grace.' Fung, *The Epistle to the Galatians*, (Eerdmans,1988) footnote 62 p.163

[5] *The Dictionary of New Testament Theology* Volume 2 (Paternoster Press Revised Edition) p.444

[6] Fung, *Galatians* p.164

[7] *Dictionary of Jesus and the Gospels* (IVP, 1992) p.457

[8] Romans 10:4 describes Christ as the 'end of the law.'

[9] D.A. Carson *The Expositor's Bible Commentary* Matthew (Zondervan,1995) p.146

[10] Carson p.140

[11] J.R.W. Stott Bible Speaks Today *Romans* (IVP,1994) p.222

[12] Michael Scott Horton *The Law of Perfect Freedom* (Moody Press,1993) p.26

[13] Simon Austen *Why Should God Bother with me?* (Christian Focus Publications, 2002)

[14] R.T.France *Matthew Evangelist and Teacher* (Paternoster Press, 1989) p.196

6

A Better Provision

I write from the comfort of a warm study. I am well fed and clothed. I have a place to sleep and no fear of a lack of provisions for tomorrow. Many of those reading these words will share my comfort – few of us will experience the horror and desperation of not knowing where our next meal will come from.

Perhaps it is for this reason that we find it difficult to identify with the people of Israel. As they wandered in the desert they looked through the rose-tinted spectacles of the past to the time when they were in Egypt, able to enjoy fine produce and gastronomic luxury. Now, freed by the grace of God from the slavery that went with such indulgence and wandering in the desert, they grumble.

> In the desert the whole community grumbled against Moses and Aaron. The Israelites said to them, 'If only we had died by the LORD's hand in Egypt! There we sat round pots of meat and ate all the food we wanted, but you have brought us out into this desert to starve this entire assembly to death.' (Exodus 16:2)

How quickly they had forgotten their past – their cries to God as they experienced the pain of slavery; their questions about his covenant promises with Abraham. Their prayers had been answered, but their memories were short, for now they grumble, complaining to the

Lord who had rescued them and miraculously freed them from their bondage in Egypt. Yet the same God who heard their cries then and graciously rescued them is the same God who hears their grumbles now and graciously provides for them. In doing so he not only meets their needs, but also tests them, to 'see whether they will follow my instructions.' (Exodus 16:4). God's provision of bread and water and the test of faithfulness that accompanies it teach us about his greatest provision of all, the Lord Jesus Christ, and how in him the solution to their failure, and ours, can be found.

The provision of bread

It was never going to be easy to live in the desert. A vast people had been freed by the miraculous intervention of God. They had seen his provision and had experienced his power. That in itself should have been enough to give them the confidence that he would provide for their needs whilst they travelled to the land he had promised. If the powers of Egypt could not stop God's purposes, then neither could hunger in the wilderness. Yet the people did not speak to Moses because they trusted God's provision, but because they were angered at the apparent lack of it.

It was in the midst of such foolish rebellion that God provided manna, a bread-like food which they were to eat throughout their years of wandering in the desert. This bread sustained them physically, but it also taught them spiritually as it reminded them of their dependence on God both for life and law.

The dependence for life
Without the manna, the people would have died before they arrived at the promised land. God's daily provision

was essential if they were to experience what God had promised to Abraham. And so 'The people were shown God's unfailing provision . . God's feeding them with manna . . . graphically portrayed the truth that life is God's gift and that his children are given bread from heaven by their father.'[1] God cared for the people he had chosen and he showed his care by providing for their physical needs.

The dependence for law

The provision of bread was not simply a physical necessity which reminded the people of a spiritual dependence. It was also given to teach them that life does not consist of bread alone. The manna was given not only so that their bellies would be full but also to humble them, to test their hearts and to remind them of their dependence on God's word in every area of life. God wanted to teach them that just as bread is essential for physical well-being, so God's word is essential for spiritual well-being.

> He humbled you, causing you to hunger and then feeding you with manna, which neither you nor your fathers had known, to teach you that man does not live on bread alone but on every word that comes from the mouth of the LORD. (Deuteronomy 8:3)

It was for this reason that the 'bread' of God became thought of as the law he had given to his people for their holiness and spiritual nourishment. 'In fact, it was commonly thought that the real manna which gives life is the living word of the instruction of the Torah.'[2] (The Old Testament Law)

The picture of bread in the Old Testament teaches that God is concerned about and provides for our physical nourishment. But it also teaches us that he is more concerned for our spiritual nourishment – for even that which was given to meet the needs of a hungry people was given to teach those same people to rely on God's word.

The true bread from heaven

We may learn two great lessons from the Old Testament, but it also presents us with two great problems. The first is that even those who ate manna died one day – it could not sustain 'life' forever. The second is that the people to whom the law was given repeatedly broke that law and rebelled against the lawgiver. Manna alone was not enough to provide for the real needs of humanity.

By the first century AD, manna had taken on another level of spiritual significance in the minds of many. Later rabbis had begun to teach that when the Messiah came, manna would once again fall on the Passover[3] and with the political climate as it was, there was a renewed search for the kingly deliverer who would free Israel from its Roman oppression.

Then one day, near the Passover festival, Jesus performed a spectacular miracle. From a small packed lunch he fed an enormous crowd, numbered by the men present as 5000 but with women and children perhaps up to 20000.[4] The crowd was amazed. Could this be 'the prophet' for whom they had waited these long years since Moses had prophesied and promised his arrival?[5] They followed Jesus, eager for a miracle to prove who he was – if Moses provided manna, what would this man give?

But Jesus would not perform to order. Rather than proving his identity or confirming their misconceptions with a miracle, he proclaimed a radical truth about himself which surpassed that of manna in the wilderness and provided the solution to man's greatest need. He said:

> I tell you the truth, it is not Moses who has given you the bread from heaven, but it is my Father who gives you the true bread from heaven. For the bread of God is he who comes down from heaven and gives life to the world . . . I am the bread of life. He who comes to me will never go hungry, and he who believes in me will never be thirsty. (John 6:32,33,35)

Manna was a picture of God's gracious provision for his people and a reminder to them that life consists in more than bread alone. Here Jesus declares that *he* is God's greatest provision – the true bread who comes down from heaven – and that by coming to him and believing in him, it is possible to have eternal life. Manna brought physical sustenance, but all those who ate of it still died. Jesus brings spiritual sustenance, fulfilling the law that we could never keep and providing for us in such a way that through faith in him we would have eternal life. Whereas manna is the 'corruptible food of the belly, [Jesus is] true food for the soul.'[6]

The Provision of Water

The people of God did not only grumble at their apparent lack of food. They also grumbled at the inadequate supply of water to quench their thirst.

> [The Israelite community] camped at Rephidim, but there was no water for the people to drink. So they quarrelled with Moses and said, 'Give us water to drink.' Moses replied 'Why do you quarrel with me?

Why do you put the LORD to the test.' (Exodus 17:1b,2)

It is interesting to note that whereas bread was provided as a test for the people, their complaints about water and the provision that resulted is presented to the reader of the Old Testament as 'putting the Lord to the test.' No additional comment is made in the text about how God viewed the people even though they were, once again, showing their lack of faith and trust in their redeemer.

Moses is simply told to take the staff which he had used to strike the Nile and to hit the rock at Horeb, from which water would then flow to assuage the thirst of the desperate people. And so 'Yahweh's presence results once more in the provision for a complaining people.'[7]

What perhaps is more unusual is the second account in the Old Testament of this same provision. (Numbers 20). Once again there was no water and once again the people grumble against Moses. This time the Lord said to Moses, 'Take the staff, and you and your brother Aaron gather the assembly together. Speak to that rock before their eyes and it will pour out its water.' (Numbers 20:8).

The problem was that Moses did not follow God's instructions. Rather than speaking to the rock, he struck the rock with his staff in order to provide water for the grumbling people. But the consequence of *striking* the rock rather than *speaking* to the rock was catastrophic for Moses. God said, 'Because you did not trust in me enough to honour me as holy in the sight of the Israelites, you will not bring this community into the land I give them.' (Numbers 20:12)

Moses had been called by God to lead the people from slavery to the promised land, but now, as a result of striking the rock rather than speaking to the rock, he was to die in the wilderness. His years of faithfulness crushed in one rash action.

It all seems rather harsh. Why was it that the faithful Moses should suffer such a great punishment when time and time again the people rebelled and were forgiven? This rock must be more than the source of water and its meaning must be deeper than that of thirst-quenching provision.

'That rock was Christ'

When warning the church in Corinth about their rather wayward lifestyle, the apostle Paul used the picture of God's provision in the wilderness to teach them. As he did so he spoke of the rock that accompanied them as Christ himself.

> They drank from the spiritual rock that accompanied them, and that rock was Christ. (1 Corinthians 10:4)

The people drank water from a rock because they were thirsty, but in doing so we learn something about the Lord Jesus Christ and what it means to live as a Christian.

In the Old Testament God was frequently spoken of as 'the rock'.[8] This might provide us with a clue both to the problem Moses faced in Numbers 20 and the way in which Christ, the rock, is a 'better provision' for us. In his book *The Unfolding Mystery*, Clowney has suggested that in Numbers 20, Moses' action was in effect to strike God, the rock. Before Moses left Egypt, his staff had been used to strike the river Nile and turn it to blood – a clear 'act of judgement' on those who were rebelling against the God of Israel. Therefore when Moses struck the rock in disobedience he was, according to Clowney, exercising judgement on God, effectively putting him on trial for the difficulties he had brought upon Moses. Water came from the rock not only to provide for the needs of the people but also as a picture of judgement on Moses for his disobedience before God.

Whether Clowney is right or not, two Biblical truths flow from this picture. The first is that God is holy. Moses had publicly disobeyed God before the people, abusing his holiness and taking the consequence for doing so. In his actions we 'are reminded of the holiness of God and the sinfulness of men – and the need for faithful obedience.'[9]

We are also reminded of the one who ultimately took God's judgement on our behalf – the one from whom living waters flow, Jesus Christ. In John's gospel Jesus twice refers to water in connection with himself. The first time is in conversation with a Samaritan woman who had come to a well to collect water. It was rather strange that Jesus was speaking with her at all. He was a man, she was a woman. He was a Jew, she was not. What is more, she had come to collect water at midday, unlike the majority of women who would have come either in the morning or the evening, when it could have been cooler – a sign, perhaps, that she was also a social outcast. If Jesus can provide for her, then Jesus can provide for anyone, whatever their social status or stigma.

In the conversation that followed, Jesus spoke of living water that would be given by Jesus and would result in eternal life.

> Whoever drinks the water I give him will never thirst.
> Indeed, the water I give him will become in him a
> spring of water welling up to eternal life. (John 4:14)

The Old Testament's use of 'water' is rich and varied[10] and a detailed study would not be appropriate here. What is important is that water is identified with Jesus and faith in him. He quenches real thirst; that is, spiritual thirst.

In the second passage in John's Gospel, Jesus stands up on the 'last and greatest day of the feast' (a feast which included a dramatic water-pouring ceremony) and said:

> If anyone is thirsty, let him come to me and drink.
> (John 7:37b)

One of the principal aims of the festival at which Jesus said these words, (The Feast of Tabernacles) was to remember the provision of God in the wilderness. At the end of the month of celebrations the people were led in an extended prayer of praise and confession which included a reminder of God's provision of bread and water. Interestingly in John's Gospel, Jesus has shown in chapter 6 that he is a 'better bread' than the manna, just as he shows in chapter seven that he is a 'better drink' than the water from the rock.

One final thought from John's gospel may be sufficient to draw this all too brief chapter to a close. In John 19 we read of the death of Jesus on the cross. As with the Passover lamb of Exodus, the bones of Jesus are not broken. And as with the Passover lamb, the death of Jesus 'absorbs' the wrath of God so that those who believe may be free to enter the true promised land of heaven. In order to be certain of his death the soldiers pierced Jesus' side with a spear 'bringing a sudden flow

of blood and water.' (John 19:34). We shall see elsewhere
how Old Testament imagery and history might explain
what is going on here, but it could be that the picture
presented to us by Clowney has something to say at this
point. Jesus the rock is 'struck' by the judgement of God
and once that has happened, water flows from his side.
In doing so he takes the wrath of God from us, thereby
enabling us to be forgiven and accepted for eternal life.
Whatever we make of Clowney's suggestion, there is
no doubt that in his death, Jesus the rock takes our
judgement and thereby provides for us a provision of
'living water' that is sufficient for eternal life.

It is therefore Jesus Christ himself who is the
provision of God and the sustenance of God as we 'travel'
to heaven. He is the true bread and the living water. We
need nothing more than his forgiveness, his rescue and
his Spirit to sustain us as God's people. Jesus is our 'better
provision.'

NOTES:

[1] Edmund Clowney *The Unfolding Mystery* (Navipress,
1988) p.117

[2] Lesslie Newbigin *The Light Has Come, An Exposition
of the Fourth Gospel* (The Handsel Press Limited, 1982)
p.80

[3] 'Toward the end of the third century AD, Rabbi Isaac
argued that 'as the former redeemer cause manna to
descend . . so will the latter Redeemer cause manna to
descend.' Perhaps the same sentiment coursed through
some circles in the first century.' D.A. Carson *The Gospel
According to John* (IVP,1991) p.271

[4] Carson, p.270

[5] In Deuteronomy 18:15 Moses had promised a 'prophet like him.'

[6] *Calvin's Commentaries* Volume XX (Baker Book House,1996) p.315

[7] John Durham, Word Biblical Commentary Volume 3, *Exodus* (Word, 1987) p.231

[8] E.g. Psalm 18:2; 31:3; 42:9; Deuteronomy 32:30,32

[9] Gordon Wenham Tyndale Old Testament Commentaries *Numbers* (IVP,1981,1993 reprint) p.151

[10] Isaiah 12:3; 49:3 relates water to salvation; the pouring out of the Spirit will be like pouring water on thirsty land, Isaiah 44:3; God will make an everlasting covenant with those who come to the 'waters', Isaiah 55:3f; There is also some evidence for waters being associated with the law.

7

A Better Sacrifice

When we talk about 'sacrifice' in the modern world we do not often think about the shedding of blood. For us, sacrifice means giving something up or taking something on. We might hear someone say what a sacrifice it was to give up a job for the sake of a family, or to take on the responsibility of visiting an elderly aunt. It is a far cry from the picture of sacrifice in the Bible – for there sacrifice was instituted to achieve something. It had an end point and was not a virtue in and of itself. The bloody reality of a screaming animal being butchered on an altar was not a task to impress the neighbours or make one feel better. It was a very real reminder of the severity of sin and the need for God's forgiveness.

If you have read the last few chapters of this book, you will be no stranger to the spiritual implications of a slaughtered animal. At the Passover the blood of the lamb that was smeared on the doorposts and lintels of the houses in Egypt was a powerful reminder of the consequence of God's wrath and significance of the freedom he won for his people. Likewise, the covenant ceremony in Exodus involved the shedding of blood and the sprinkling of that blood on those assembled before the altar. In agreeing to fulfil the conditions of the law, the people were putting themselves under the judgement of God, agreeing that their lives should be 'sacrificed' if they failed to do what they had promised.

The sacrifices of the Old Testament do not stop there. Anyone who has read the book of Leviticus will be overwhelmed by the description of a host of sacrifices instituted for the people as they travelled across the desert. Broadly speaking, these sacrifices related to two aspects of God's revelation. The first is that people are created for a relationship with God. He provides and sustains life and in response the people made 'peace' and 'fellowship' offerings, burnt offerings and celebrated three annual festivals of harvest thanksgiving. The second group of sacrifices reflect the fact that those who were created to be in relationship with God did not and do not live in a relationship with God. They have 'sinned' and need that sin to be dealt with if the relationship with God is to be restored.

The five main types of offering, as seen in Leviticus chapters 1 to 7, were the burnt offering, the cereal offering, the peace offering, the sin offering and the guilt offering. The only offering which did not consist of flesh and blood was the cereal offering of grain and oil. For this reason it was often made in association with the others, all of which involved a basic ritual.

First the worshipper brought the offering (an animal) to the temple, laid hands upon it and killed it. The only sacrifices not performed by the worshipper were the national offerings (such as the Day of Atonement), which we shall look at in due course. Once the sins had been confessed with the laying on of hands and the animal had been slaughtered, the blood was 'manipulated' by the priest, collected in a basin and sprinkled on the sides of the altar. The remaining blood was poured out at the base of the altar and the remaining portions of the sacrifice were eaten in a sacrificial meal.

In each sacrifice the principle of substitution is present. The sacrificial animal replaces the sinful human being. It dies in the place of the sinner. This sacrificial system was not man-made but instituted by God. 'Individual sacrifices are not a human device to placate God but a means of atonement provided by God himself.'[1] Although the notion of sacrifice may be far from the modern mind, we ignore it at our peril, for it shows how severe sin is in God's eyes and what enormous care he must have for his people if he instituted a means of dealing with it. It is because God is holy and loving that he wants to deal with our sin. Without sacrifice, we would perish before a holy God, totally unable to save ourselves. Sacrifices are therefore 'The fruit of grace, not its root.'[2]

We see the two sides of sacrifice – the severity of sin and the grace of God – most clearly on the day of Atonement, which we read about in Leviticus 16.

The Day of Atonement

If the Passover secured redemption and the Covenant demarcated the people as God's people, the Day of Atonement dealt with their sin. It was the highest day in the Jewish Calendar, during which Jews abstained from all earthly pleasures. Only the high priest could officiate at this ceremony. First he sacrificed a bull for his own sin. Wearing the linen garments which symbolized purity and humility, he took some of the blood of the sacrifice and entered the Holy of Holies. This central part of the temple was the place where God symbolically dwelt. No-one could enter this inner sanctuary except the high priest, and then only on this most holy of days. Once inside he sprinkled incense on the hot coals of the censer he carried with him, creating a cloud to protect him from the presence of God. Blood was then sprinkled on the atonement cover (the golden lid of the ark which was located in the Holy of Holies), and before the atonement cover seven times.

Once he had made the sacrifice for his own sins he then took one of two goats and sacrificed it for the people's sin and repeated the rite he had performed with the bull's blood. Following this, blood was then smeared in other parts of the temple to purify it for future worship.

There remained one other goat, selected by lot for the ceremony. This goat was not sacrificed. Instead the high priest laid both his hands on its head and confessed the sins of the people. The goat was then sent into the wilderness, carrying the sins of the people far away. This 'scapegoat' then died in the wilderness, outside the camp, many miles from the people. 'This ritual was to provide visual representation to the assembly of the reality that in this day their sins had been completely wiped out and the power of these sins was terminated forever.'[3]

Nowadays we might scoff at the apparent barbarism of these acts. But we must be very wary of doing so. The New Testament and the death of Jesus in particular will not allow us to reject the sacrifices of the Old Testament without also redefining the character of God.

The Completed sacrifice

Just before Jesus died on the cross, John tells us that he cried out, 'It is finished.' (John 19:30). There, outside the city wall, Jesus' work and mission found their completion. Throughout his ministry he had made it clear that he would die. The gospels have a geographical and theological direction which point to the cross and the blood which Jesus shed. As we contemplate its meaning, we cannot but avoid the fact that 'The interpretation of Christ's death as a sacrifice is embedded in every important type of New Testament teaching.'[4]

It is the Day of Atonement in particular which sheds light on Jesus' sacrificial death and what it means for us. For 'every aspect of the work of atonement discerned in the complex model of that ancient festival [the day of Atonement] finds its fulfilment in him.'[5]

The Problem of sin

The Day of Atonement would not have been needed unless sin was a real problem. If we have a low view of sin (that it does not really matter), or a low view of the holiness of God (that he doesn't really mind about sin), then we need to read Leviticus 16. So serious is sin that four different words are used in that chapter to describe the magnitude of mankind's uncleanness and rebellion. Derek Tidball, in writing of the significance of this chapter in Leviticus, sums up the problem confronting humanity: 'This holy God has been offended by his people; and the offence cannot be ignored, for that would compromise his purity and character. The offence must be removed, it won't just go away; it must be taken away.'[6]

What the Day of Atonement provided was a spiritual spring-clean when sins could be removed and people's relationship with God could be restored. The cleaning agent God had prescribed to achieve this purification was blood.

The importance of blood

> For the life of a creature is in the blood, and I have
> given it to you to make atonement for yourselves
> on the altar; it is the blood that makes atonement
> for one's life. (Leviticus 17:11)

God makes it very clear. If people are to be put right
with God, forgiven and restored in relationship with
him, free from the condemnation of their sin (which is
what atonement means), then blood needs to be shed.
This shedding of blood symbolizes a life laid down on
behalf of others. 'The focus rests on the death of the
victim as the significant aspect of the sacrifice; that is a
life given in exchange for a life . . . blood was the price
to be paid if cleansing and forgiveness were to be
available.'[7] Once the blood had been shed and the life
had been given, then the perfect payment had been made.

The only problem with the Day of Atonement was
that it had to be repeated. It couldn't deal with sin once
and for all because the sacrifice could not be a perfect
substitute. An animal could never stand in the place of
humankind, the pinnacle of God's creation. Only man
could make atonement for man, but only God could
take the initiative to bring about that atonement. Hence
our need for Jesus, the God-man, who 'came into the
world to save sinners' (1 Timothy 1:15) and whose life
was given as a 'ransom for many' (Mark 10:45).

The Old Testament blood sacrifices could only be
shadows, pointers to a greater reality found in Christ.
Only his blood was and is sufficient to deal with our
sin. We have already seen that Christ is our Passover
lamb. We have already seen that he is the sacrifice who
initiated the New Covenant; but he is also the sacrificial

goat and the scapegoat, whose death brought final and total forgiveness. When Jesus died, the curtain which separated the Holy of Holies from the rest of the temple ripped in two from top to bottom – from God to man[8]. The people now had access to God because a once-for-all sacrifice had been made, on the cross, outside the city wall. In his death, Jesus fulfilled all sacrifice. He was for us the perfect sacrifice. 'In the New Testament Jesus' death fulfilled the entire intent of the Day of Atonement . . .his death consummated the entire Old Testament sacrificial system.'[9]

The sacrificed goat

The two goats that were used on the Day of Atonement shed light on the nature of Jesus' sacrifice. Both were vital for the process of forgiveness and purity.

Of the two goats required, the first was sacrificed as a substitute for the people whose sin it symbolically carried. It was a sacrifice of *propitiation* – a term we may have often used without understanding the full implications of what it means. To put it simply, 'to propitiate somebody means to placate his or her anger.'[10] God is angry at sin and that anger finds its expression in sacrifice.

Contrary to the popular picture of a God who is so loving that sin doesn't seem to matter, the God of the Bible is a Holy God before whom our sin matters a great deal. It is not simply a blockage between creator and created. It is also an object of wrath. Without that wrath being dealt with, the sinner is in peril of hell, bound for a Godless eternity. In providing a sacrificial system, God has taken the initiative to deal with that wrath. He directs it to another, a substitute, who takes the consequence of God's wrath (death) in our place.

The sacrifice of a goat was therefore a very visual reminder of the need for propitiation. But it is only a reminder, because 'it is impossible for the blood of bulls and goats to take away sin.' (Hebrews 10:4). The sacrifices of the Old Testament point us forward to the perfect sacrifice of sin which results in perfect propitiation.

In his letter to the Romans, the apostle Paul spends from 1:18 to 3:20 explaining that 'all are sinners and subject to his wrath.'[11] He then goes on to show how that wrath has been dealt with in Christ.

> God presented him as a sacrifice of atonement, through faith in his blood. He did this to demonstrate his justice, because in his forbearance he had left the sins committed beforehand unpunished. (Romans 3:25a)

Whilst some have debated exactly what Paul meant by the phrase 'sacrifice of atonement,' the consensus seems to be that this refers to the propitiation in his sacrificial death. In other words, when Jesus died he was placing himself under the wrath of God – sacrificing himself in our place, so that the believer might be free from the consequences of the righteous anger of a holy God.

This is also seen in the first letter of John:

> This is love: not that we loved God, but that he loved us and sent his Son as an atoning sacrifice for our sins. (1 John 4:10)

The word used for 'atoning sacrifice' is the Greek word *hilasmos*. This is found almost universally in the Greek version of the Old Testament to refer to the removal of sin through sacrifice. Therefore 'There can be little doubt then that when the author uses the term *hilasmos* here he is emphasizing that God sent Jesus Christ to be an atoning sacrifice to remove the guilt we had incurred because of our sins so that we might have eternal life.'[12]

John tells us that God took this initiative to deal with our sin because he loves us. Unlike any pagan equivalent sacrifice in the ancient world, the Old Testament sacrifices were not made to appease God's anger but initiated by God to absorb it. The outrage we might feel at a God who can become angry is silenced when we understand that it is that same God who has graciously taken the steps to deal with that righteous anger himself.

The scapegoat

The function of the second goat also finds its fulfilment in Jesus. If the first goat was a sacrifice of propitiation, the second was one of *expiation*. Although some translations of the Bible prefer to use this word instead of propitiation, it has a different meaning and sheds another light on the cross. Expiation can be thought of in these terms: 'If sin is a thing, blotted out, cast from us, and the like, then we properly talk of expiation.'[13]

We have seen that sin cannot simply be blotted out – God's wrath will not allow it. But that does not mean sin is not 'removed.' On the contrary, the Bible often speaks of sin being dealt with in this way.[14] Here is where the destiny of the second goat illuminates our understanding. The scapegoat symbolically carried the sins of the people away from the place where God dwelt. It passed through the camp and out into the wilderness, thereby removing the barrier between God and his people.

In the same way, Jesus bore our sin as the goat did.[15] And in the same way, Jesus died 'outside the camp,' in that he died away from the temple, outside the city.[16] Jesus therefore acted as a sacrifice of propitiation (in that he dealt with the wrath of God from us) *and* a sacrifice of expiation (in that he removed our sin from us).

The glorious news for the New Testament believer is that the sacrifice of Jesus does not need to be repeated. Unlike the sacrifice on the annual Day of Atonement, Jesus died once for all, providing a complete satisfaction for the sins of the whole world. And so 'The sufficient sacrifice of Christ in conformity to the will of God created the new situation for the worshipping community in which every obstacle to fellowship with God has been effectively removed.'[17]

A better sacrifice has been made. Every obstacle has been removed. We have been declared as righteous through the atoning blood of Jesus. We are free to offer a different sacrifice – the sacrifice of a holy life as a response to God's wonderful and gracious initiative.

Therefore, I urge you, brothers, in view of God's mercy, to offer your bodies as living sacrifices, holy and pleasing to God – this is your spiritual act of worship (Romans 12:1).

NOTES:

[1] J.R.W. Stott *The Cross of Christ* (IVP, 1986) p.138
[2] R.J.Thompson Sacrifice *The Illustrated Bible Dictionary* (Tyndale,1980) p.1366
[3] John E. Hartley Word Biblical Commentary Volume 4 *Leviticus,* (Word, 1992) p.237

[4] Thomas Crawford *Doctrine of the Holy Scripture respecting the Atonement* (Wm Blackwood 1871 5th Edition, 1888) p.453-454

[5] Derek Tidball Bible Speaks Today *The Message of the Cross* (IVP, 2001) p.84

[6] Ibid, p.71

[7] Ibid, p.76

[8] Matthew 27:51; Mark 15:38

[9] John E. Hartley Word Biblical Commentary Volume 4 *Leviticus,* (Word, 1992) p.238

[10] J.R.W. Stott The Bible Speaks Today *Romans* (IVP, 1994) p.113

[11] Leon Morris *The Epistle to the Romans* (IVP Eerdmans, 1988) p.180

[12] Colin G. Kruse *The Letters of John* (Eerdmans Apollos, 2000) p.161

[13] Leon Morris *The Illustrated Bible Dictionary* (Tyndale, 1980) p.491

[14] e.g Psalm 103:12 'As far as the east is from the west, so far has he removed our transgressions from us.'

[15] 2 Corinthians 5:21; Hebrews 9:28; 1 Peter 2:24

[16] e.g. John 19:17; Hebrews 13:12

[17] William L. Lane Word Biblical Commentary Volume 47a *Hebrews 1-8,* (Word,1991) p.270

8

A Better Priest

J. C. Ryle, the famous nineteenth century Bishop of Liverpool, wrote a book entitled *Knots Untied*. It had the lengthy subtitle of *being plain statements on disputed points in religion from the standpoint of an Evangelical Churchman*. In it Ryle began his chapter on 'priesthood' with these words:

> He that wishes to have any comfort in religion must have a priest. A religion without a priest is a poor, unhappy, useless thing. Now what is our religion? Do we have a priest?[1]

I wonder what comes into our minds as we read those words? Do we picture a clergyman, dressed in clerical robes and reassuring the burdened sinner that his transgressions have been forgiven? Or do we think of the 'eucharistic' celebrant investing bread and wine with a spiritual significance they would not otherwise have?

Ryle would have been shocked at either conclusion – and would have been grieved at the depth of the confusion which might cause us to make such assumptions. For there is only one true priest – the Lord Jesus Christ himself. The New Testament spells out for us the nature of his priesthood, but to understand it in its fullness, we need, once again, to grasp the Old Testament teaching about this much misunderstood office. In this chapter we will look at the pattern of priesthood, the problems of priesthood and the perfect priesthood.

The Pattern of Priesthood

The Old Testament priest was no minor character on the fringe of mainstream society. He was central to the life and spiritual wellbeing of the people. Without him there would have been no confidence that forgiveness of sins was possible. Without him there would have been no representative of humanity before a holy God. Priesthood was important – and no aspect of priesthood was more important than the office of High Priest. His responsibilities and his qualifications were fundamental, not only to the people's standing before God, but also to our understanding of the person and work of Jesus.

Responsibilities

The chief responsibility of the high priest was to offer the sacrifice on the Day of Atonement. Having made a sacrifice for his own sins, he would then act as the peoples' representative, standing before the mercy seat of God in the Temple, shrouded with the cloud of incense to protect him from laying eyes on the holy dwelling place of Yahweh. Only he could enter this inner sanctuary; only he could make the sacrifice for the sins of the people; only he could purify the Temple for future worship. In every way 'his greatest task was the absolution of the community on the Day of Atonement.'[2]

As the peoples' representative before God, he was also their intercessor, providing access to God through sacrifice and then articulating on their behalf their prayers of penitence and shame. Without the high priest they would be lost, unable to approach God, cut off by their sin and unsure of their salvation.

The High Priest was therefore the 'highest representative of the people.'[3] But as such the qualifications required to take on the job were very stringent.

Qualifications

Those selected for the job of High Priest had to be from the tribe of Levi and physically descended from the original High Priest, Aaron (on their Father's side). The post was by divine appointment and therefore anyone assuming the role without divine commission or correct ancestry, was liable to the death penalty.

> The Lord said to Aaron . . . Only you and your sons may serve as priests in connection with everything at the altar and inside the curtain. I am giving you the service of the priesthood as a gift. Anyone else who comes near the sanctuary must be put to death. (Numbers 18:7)

At the same time, the High Priest needed to be able to identify with the people. He needed to be one of them, their representative rather than their master, perfect in form (Leviticus 21:16-23) but human in nature. This then is the pattern of priesthood – a man, descended from Aaron, of the tribe of Levi, commissioned by God; a sacrificial mediator and an intercessor for the people.

The Problems of Priesthood

Although the Old Testament priesthood required rigorous standards, there were still fundamental and unavoidable problems relating both to the priest's qualifications and his office. The credentials, the service and the location of ministry were all flawed and therefore insufficient to provide the ultimate solution to the problem of human sin.

His credentials were weak

Before the High Priest was in a position to make a sacrifice on behalf of the people, he had to make a sacrifice for his own sins. Despite his high office, he was not qualified to enter the presence of God as he stood. His sin was too serious. However righteous he was in his own eyes or the eyes of others, he was not righteous in the eyes of God. Nothing excused him from the requirement of sacrifice. Day after day, year after year, he needed to make sacrifices. He could not stand before a Holy God with any confidence without the blood of a sacrificial animal to atone for his sin.

Not only that, but his ministry was finite. One day he would die; one day his office would be taken over by another. A new mediator would then be required to perform the same functions of intercession and sacrifice on behalf of the people.

The Old Testament Levitical priesthood was therefore imperfect, weakened by the sin of the office holder.

His service was inadequate

A perfect sacrifice would perfectly and completely deal with sin, but the High Priest of the Old Testament had to make repeated sacrifices. Every year on the Day of Atonement he would make a sacrifice for his own sins and then for the sins of others. All he could hope to do was to make those who stood before him outwardly or ceremonially clean.

The blood of goats and bulls and the ashes of a heifer sprinkled on those who are ceremonially unclean sanctify them so that they are outwardly clean. (Hebrews 9:13)

Just as the priest was inadequate because of his sin, so the sacrifice he made was insufficient. He could identify with the people as a sinner well enough, but the blood of the sacrifice could not completely deal with that sin. His own humanity prevented the perfection of his service. At best the sacrifice was an outward cleansing and an annual reminder of the severity of sin which weakened the service he performed. Although he needed to be able to identify with the people, neither he nor the sacrifice he made was sufficient for perfection. His service was inadequate.

His place was imperfect

When the people were travelling in the wilderness and before the temple was built in Jerusalem under Solomon, the sacrifices were made at the tabernacle. It was a tented structure with the same basic features that later appeared in the temple. At its heart was the inner sanctuary, the holy of holies, into which the High Priest ventured on the Day of Atonement. God had given very careful instructions about the construction of both the tabernacle and the Temple. This was the means by which God would symbolically dwell among his people. This was the place where sinful humanity would find forgiveness and reconciliation.

It was however only a shadow of the reality. The real place of God's throne is in heaven and therefore the real tabernacle or temple is not on earth. We not only have an imperfect priest offering an imperfect service, we also have an imperfect sanctuary.

The Old Testament leaves us with a clear picture of the nature of both sin and sacrifices. It presents us with a thorough-going but inadequate priesthood operating in a Temple which is only a shadow of reality. It causes us once again to lift our eyes to a different horizon and to search for a better priest.

The Perfect Priesthood

In the New Testament, Jesus is presented to us as the perfect High Priest. Picking up the themes and features of the Old Testament, the writer to the Hebrews explains how Jesus is the perfect priest who has offered a perfect sacrifice and now ministers at a perfect sanctuary.

Jesus' priestly qualifications
Just as with the High Priest in the Old Testament, Jesus was appointed by divine commission. In comparing the nature of the Old Testament appointment with that of Jesus, the writer to the Hebrews tells us that Jesus did not assume this office himself, but was granted it by the Father:

> No-one takes this honour upon himself; he must be called by God, just as Aaron was. So Christ also did not take upon himself the glory of becoming a high priest. But God said to him: You are my son; today I have become your Father. (Hebrews 5:4-5)

So far so good. Jesus holds the same credentials as that of the Old Testament office. But thereafter the paths diverge. Those of us who can readily recall the Christmas stories will be aware that Jesus is not of the tribe of Levi, as was required for Old Testament priesthood, but of the tribe of Judah. Here Jesus' qualifications would appear to preclude him from office. Strictly speaking it means that he cannot be a priest, and that should he try to do so, he is liable to the death penalty.

It is these issues which are addressed by the writer to the Hebrews. In order to show that nature and validity of Jesus' priesthood, the writer explains that Jesus does not follow the Levitical order but that of Melchizedek.

We first find Melchizedek in Genesis 14:17-20. There, as a 'priest of God Most High' (Genesis 14:18), he blessed Abraham after the latter's victory over Kedorlaomer. Abraham responded by giving Melchizedek a tenth of all the plunder.

After this rather brief encounter with the patriarch, Melchizedek 'receded into the shadows of history.'[4] Thereafter he does not appear again until Psalm 110:4

The Lord has sworn
And will not change his mind:
'You are a priest for ever in the order of Melchizedek.'

At this point in the history of Israel (when the Psalm was written) the Levitical priesthood had been in operation for about 350 years – and yet it is this verse which the writer of the Hebrews uses to validate and explain the nature of Christ's priesthood. Having confirmed that Jesus was divinely appointed in accordance with priestly requirements he then goes on to explain that Jesus was in fact 'designated by God to be high priest in the order of Melchizedek.' (Hebrews 5:6-10).

The nature of this priestly order is extremely important for understanding why the priesthood of Jesus is superior to that which it replaces.

First, Melchizedek appears in scripture with no beginning and no end. In that sense, his priesthood is permanent and not restricted by the death of the office holder.

> Without father or mother, without genealogy, without beginning of days or end of life, like the Son of God he remains a priest forever. (Hebrews 7:3)

Secondly, the activity of Melchizedek shows that Jesus is greater than the entire Levitical order. The argument runs something like this: If Melchizedek blessed Abraham and Abraham 'submitted' to his kingly rule and priestly office, then it follows that those who come from the body of Abraham (that is, his descendants, which included the Levites) are also in submission, or inferior to, Melchizedek. Such is the argument in Hebrews 7.

> Just think how great he was: Even the patriarch Abraham gave him a tenth of the plunder! Now the law requires the descendants of Levi who become priests to collect a tenth from the people – that is, their brothers – even though their brothers are descended from Abraham. This man, however, did not trace his descent from Levi, yet he collected a tenth from Abraham and blessed him who had the promises. And without doubt the lesser person is blessed by the greater. In the one case, the tenth is collected by men who die; but in the other case, by him who is declared to be living. One might even say that Levi, who collects the tenth, paid the tenth

through Abraham, because when Melchizedek met Abraham, Levi was still in the body of his ancestor. (Hebrews 7:4-10)

In this way, the priesthood of Jesus is superior to Levitical priesthood – it is permanent and it is primary. Thus although Jesus is from the tribe of Judah, he can still be the perfect high priest without being inconsistent with the scriptures that preceded him. After all, 'The Messiah would not disregard Old Testament law and attempt to get himself installed illegally as a high priest in Aaron's line.'[5]

Jesus' priestly service

Jesus' credentials show him to be a superior high priest by virtue of his permanence and his primacy. But two other aspects of his priesthood make him the 'ultimate priest.'

The first is that he was perfect. Unlike the High Priests of the Old Testament, Jesus did not need to make a sacrifice for his own sins before he could offer a sacrifice on behalf of the people – he was 'holy, blameless, pure, set apart from sinners.' (Hebrews 7:26).

The second aspect of this 'better priesthood' follows on from this – he may have been perfect, but he was also personal. As a man he had experienced what we experienced – the pressures and temptations of a fallen world, the weakness and despair we feel. In that sense he could and still can identify with us, fully human, just as we are. Therefore 'We do not have a high priest who is unable to sympathise with our weaknesses, but we have one who has been tempted in every way – just as we are.' (Hebrews 4:15a). But there is of course a vast difference between Jesus as a human being and all other human beings. He was 'without sin.' (Hebrews 4:15b). We can therefore have total confidence in him. It is as Gooding has observed: 'Qualified now by his obedience and suffering, Christ has become the source of eternal salvation for all who obey him, and officially designated by God to be our high priest.'[6]

Jesus is the perfect, personal and permanent priest – who did not sacrifice a bull or a goat for sins forgiven but sacrificed himself. In doing so he opened up the gate of glory, so that all believers could approach the throne of grace with confidence. Our intercessor is permanently at hand, sinless, perfect, understanding of our humanity and its weaknesses and not requiring further sacrifice to bring us to God.

> Therefore, he is able to save completely those who come to God through him, because he always lives to intercede for them. (Hebrews 7:25)

Jesus' Priestly place
Jesus offered himself both as 'priest and victim,' as the hymn puts it. Once the final sacrifice had been made on the cross, Jesus rose again and ascended into heaven. Thereby the priestly office moved out of the shadowlands and into the reality of heaven. There, in the presence of God, the real sanctuary can be found with an open door to the throne of grace. There too, is our great high priest, interceding for us.

> When Christ came as high priest of the good things that are already here, he went through the greater and more perfect tabernacle that is not man-made. . he did not enter by means of the blood of goats and

calves; but he entered by his own blood, having obtained eternal redemption. (Hebrews 9:11-12)

There is a sense then in which Christ still holds the office of high priest. No more sacrifices are made – his was sufficient and final, but at the same time 'his work as a high priest was not finished. Seated at the right hand of God, he still retains that status and office.'[7]

So we return to Ryle's insistence that if we wish comfort in faith, we require a priest. Many, if not most, people long for a 'priest' to absolve, forgive and reassure them. J. O. Sanders observed that 'From the dawn of human history, man has craved a priest or a mediator who would represent him to God. Among men there is a universal sense that there is a God who has been offended by man's wrongdoing and who must be appeased.'[8] But there is only one who is sufficient for the task – the perfect one, who sat down at the right hand of the Father when satisfaction for sin was made through his own blood and who now, as I write and as you read, is interceding for us. Let's not remain at an earthly tabernacle nor belittle the heavenly reality. But let's trust the great high priest who sacrificed himself and entered that perfect sanctuary; the one who now serves on our behalf, to the glory of God . . . 'for we would all be lost if we did not have a high priest who constantly and incessantly intercedes for us.'[9]

NOTES
[1] J.C. Ryle *Knots Untied* (James Clarke and Co., 1977) p.192

[2] *The New International Dictonary of New Testament Theology* Volume III, Ed. Colin Brown (Paternoster, 1986) p.35

[3] *Dictionary of Theology III* p.35

[4] William L.Lane, Word Biblical Commentary Volume 47a, *Hebrews 1-8* (Word, 1991), p.cxxx

[5] David Gooding *An Unshakeable Kingdom* (IVP, 1989) p. 130

[6] Gooding p.135

[7] I. Howard Marshall *Work of Christ* (Paternoster, 1994) p.98

[8] J.O. Sanders *The Incomparable Christ* (The Moody Press, 1971 (Revised and Enlarged Edition)) p.231

[9] Gooding p.128

9

A Better Temple

Anthony Trollope presents a wonderful narrative moment as he introduces his readers to the characters of *Barchester Towers*. Mr Slope, the new Bishop's chaplain, has just preached to the assembled clergy in Barchester Cathedral. Enraged by the challenge they hear, various senior clerics rush out of the cathedral before venting their frustration in animated conversation. What is amusing is that they wait until they have left what Trollope calls 'the house of God' before doing so. They cannot behave indecently in what they perceive to be the dwelling place of God.

Although fictional and fun, that Trollopian comment is indicative of how many of us think. How often have we heard people speak of the local church 'as the house of God'? How often have we heard a parent berate an exuberant young child in church with the chilling words 'be quiet – don't you know where you are?' At the same time some Jews and Christians long for the restoration of the Temple in Jerusalem, hoping, even longing, that the glory of God will return to Zion.

In the midst of all this confusion we need to discover what the Bible says about the dwelling place of God. Does the Bible encourage us to speak about the 'house of God'? Where do we meet God in the twenty-first century?

The Tabernacle

Our story starts many years ago, as the people of God wandered in the wilderness having been released from their slavery in Egypt. Moses, the divinely appointed leader of the people, had been commanded to build a tent (known as the tent of meeting) so that God could be approached in worship. God would come to Moses in a cloud and a pillar of fire – symbols of the kingship and glory of God. (Exodus 13:21-22; 14:19-25).

After the appearance of God at Mount Sinai, this meeting place of God moved from the edge of the camp to its centre. There God lived among his people as their king. Everything about this tabernacle taught the people something about his character. Its construction, location and function, all served to instruct the people of the Old Testament about the God who had rescued them.

Structure

Exodus 25-30 devotes itself to the instructions concerning the design of the Tabernacle. It was erected at the command of God and made to the exact pattern that he gave Moses on the mountain.

> Set up the tabernacle according to the plan shown you on the mountain. (Exodus 26:30)

The outer part of the tabernacle was made from curtains of goat hair and coverings of rams skins and hides of sea cows (large aquatic animals). As one progressed towards the 'most holy place,' which was to become 'God's earthly home'[1], so the material used in its construction became more expensive and ornate. Thus the holiness of God was demonstrated by the quality of the materials used.

The courtyard was therefore made of curtains with finely twisted linen, held with bronze posts and silver hooks (Exodus 27:9-19), whereas the curtain separating the holy place from the most holy place was made of 'blue, purple and scarlet yarn and finely twisted linen, with cherubim worked into it by a skilled craftsman.' (Exodus 26:31). This curtain was to hang from gold hooks on posts of gold covered acacia wood which stood on silver bases. Behind it was the ark of testimony, a gold-covered chest with two cherubim. Here God would meet with Moses to give commands for the Israelites (Exodus 25:22).

When the tabernacle was finally completed, a cloud descended upon it and it was filled with the glory of God (Exodus 40:35-38).

Function

The tabernacle served as the portable throneroom of God.[2] This was the way in which God would dwell among his people as they travelled in the wilderness. It was 'God's earthly dwelling from Moses to David.'[3] As such, it was also the place where God would meet his people, through Moses, and later through the divinely given system of priests and sacrifices.

Location

As God's dwelling place, the tabernacle was located in the heart of the camp. Around it the tents of the various tribes of Israel were pitched, arranged again by divine instruction so that all would know their place before the king.[4]

It was just the same arrangement for all the kings of the Ancient Near East. As they would camp at the centre of the people, so God tabernacled at the centre of the people – and as the king led his army into battle, so the ark of testimony would lead the way as the people of God pursued their wilderness wanderings. And so 'the tabernacle inherited and symbolised the traditions of the Lord's glory in battle and his status as their king.'[5]

There was however one major obstacle to overcome as God dwelt among his people. As their tent-dwelling king he could identify with them and they with him and yet at the same time his tent was not open to them. They did not have the open access to God typified by the relationships of mankind before the fall. Sacrifices and priests were still required. Sin was still the problem. But the Old Testament looked forward to a time when God's tent would not simply be among them, but would be 'over' them. The earthly tabernacle clearly was not the end.

> Then the nations will know that I the LORD make Israel holy, when my sanctuary is among them for ever. (Ezekiel 37:28)

The Temple

The tabernacle remained the symbol of God's presence from the time of Moses through to the reign of David. But once enthroned and settled in his palatial surroundings, the king questioned the appropriateness of the tabernacle as a dwelling place of God.

> After the king was settled in his palace and the LORD had given him rest from all his enemies around him, he said to Nathan the prophet, 'Here I am, living in a palace of cedar, while the ark of God remains in a tent.' (2 Samuel 7:1-2)

David had it in mind to build a temple to house the ark of God but because he was stained with the blood of his enemies, the privilege of its construction went to his son, Solomon. David did, however, collect the materials, gather the treasure and buy the site (2 Samuel 24:18-25; 1 Chronicles 22:8).

Solomon's Temple

Solomon started work on the temple in the fourth year of his reign. Seven years later it was completed. As with the tabernacle, its construction and furnishings all served to teach the people about the character of God, with the most holy place, and the ark it contained, representing the very dwelling place of God on earth. Just as the glory of God had filled the tabernacle, so once completed, the glory of God filled the temple.

> When the priests withdrew from the Holy Place, the cloud filled the temple of the LORD. And the priests could not perform their service because of the cloud, for the glory of the LORD filled his temple. Then Solomon said, 'The LORD has said that he would dwell in a dark cloud; I have indeed built a magnificent temple for you, a place for you to dwell forever. (1 Kings 8:10-13)

At this stage in the history of Israel, life could not have been better. Here was the king, anointed by God, endowed with divine wisdom, having constructed a magnificent temple in which the holy creator God would dwell. God's people were in the land that he had given — and now God had made his dwelling amongst his people. Israel was a united country, basking in its blessings and parading its strength to the world. Then disaster struck.

As had happened so often in the history of Israel, the reality of human nature gripped even the most promising of kings. As Solomon grew old 'his wives turned his heart after other gods' and so the 'Lord became angry with Solomon [and said], 'Since this is your attitude and you have not kept my covenant and my decrees, which I commanded you, I will most certainly tear the kingdom away from you and give it to one of your subordinates.' (1 Kings 11:4, 11)

And so began a downward spiral. The united kingdom divided under Solomon's son; rivalry and alternative worship sites drew people away from the temple and into conflict; true worship was abandoned for arrogant and sinful indulgence and glory was exchanged for shame. Eventually the northern kingdom, known as Israel, was overtaken by the Assyrians in the eighth century BC, leaving the disobedient southerners centred on Jerusalem and the neglected temple. By the time of king Josiah, three centuries after its construction, the temple was in desperate need of repair and the people were in spiritual bankruptcy. Even their brief acts of repentance and reconstruction were insufficient to save them from ruin. In 586 B.C the might of the Babylonians overtook the feeble and godless resolve of the people. The glory of God left the most holy place, the temple was destroyed and the people carried into exile in the foreign land of Babylon.

The great dwelling place of God lay in ruins and the people and the land they had been promised were ripped apart. This was theological and political disaster on an unprecedented scale. As they licked their wounds by the waters of Babylon they asked serious questions of the nature and character of God. Was he really the all powerful, all promising God? If so, where was he now?

Ezekiel's Temple

Ezekiel was a prophet who was active in ministry during the time of the exile. In visual and dramatic ways he presented to the people of Jerusalem what would happen to them and to their temple if they carried on living without reference to their rescuing, covenant God. The arrogance of the people brought with it a presumption that all would be well and that the prophets were no more than agents of gloom, but the message they proclaimed was real enough. A covenant people needed to live a covenant life. If they did not, judgement would come. And judgement did.

Ezekiel's message is profound and terrifying. God will be God. He will act because of the honour of his name. But that same sovereign God who judges sin is the same sovereign God who restores the sinner. And so Ezekiel also contains a message of hope. The exile will not be the end. The people will return to the land and the temple will be restored.

Such is the message in the latter part of this prophet's work. In particular, we see the vision of a new temple, more wonderful than that which was destroyed, a temple from which a river would flow which sustained life; a temple which, as we shall see, finds its fulfilment in Jesus Christ.

The Second Temple

The people returned to the land full of hope and anticipation. The city was restored, the temple was rebuilt and services of repentance and law-teaching brought the people back into a covenant relationship with God – or so it seemed.

On a practical level, the temple *was* restored. Admittedly it wasn't as good as Solomon's temple and the ark never regained its position of former glory, but it did stand for nearly 500 years and it was the focus of those who lived in the land. During that time there were various threats and dangers, most notably under the reign of Antiochus Epiphanes IV (175-163BC) who set up the 'desolating statue' (a pagan altar or statue) in the most holy place, having stolen the seven-branched candelabra, the table for the showbread and the incense altar. This event provoked revolution and resulted in the temple being cleansed and restored by Maccabees in 164BC.

Despite such national fervour, the people and the temple never returned to the zenith of magnificence that had been achieved under Solomon. Sin remained a problem – a restored land and a restored temple did not bring about a restored people. Ezekiel's vision had yet to find its fulfilment.

Herod's Temple
Herod's temple was perhaps the greatest of them all. It was commenced in 19BC (arguably more for political reasons than for the glory of God) and was to surpass anything that had gone before. Throughout the lifetime of Jesus, this was the temple he would have known and experienced – a temple yet to be completed but never-the-less resplendent with glory. But it was also the temple about which Jesus prophesied destruction. And so, although completed in AD64, it was destroyed by the Romans in AD70. Its remains can still be seen in Jerusalem today.

We leave the Old Testament with Ezekiel's vision of a great temple in a restored land – a picture far from the chequered reality of the temple at the time of Jesus. But it is to Jesus we must turn if we are to find the meaning of the temple and the true fulfilment of that Old Testament ideal.

Jesus – the better tabernacle and better temple

A better tabernacle

John's gospel opens with an awe-inspiring introduction to Jesus. He is the Word, God-in-the-flesh, who came into the world. Many of us will know and love those words which we hear each year as the final reading of a traditional carol service – 'The Word became flesh and made his dwelling among us. We have seen his glory, the glory of the One and Only, who came from the Father, full of grace and truth.' (John 1:14)

Sadly for us, the translation loses some of the impact of the original. For while we can see that Jesus is the manifestation of the glory of God, just as his presence was in the tabernacle and the temple of the Old Testament, we fail to realize just what John is saying. The word which we translate as 'made his dwelling' is better translated 'tabernacled.' Here is Jesus, the God-man, tabernacling among his people and thereby manifesting God's glory to the world.

No Jewish person reading the introduction of John's gospel could fail to grasp what is being said. In the Old Testament God dwelt in the tabernacle, revealing his glory there. Now he is revealed in the person of Jesus Christ. Therefore in choosing the word 'tabernacle' 'the evangelist implies God has chosen to dwell among his people in a yet more personal way, in the Word-become flesh.'[6] Brown makes the point very clearly in his commentary on John, 'We are being told that the flesh of Jesus Christ is the new localization of God's presence on earth, and that Jesus is the replacement for the ancient tabernacle.'[7]

So where the Old Testament promises that 'in the ideal days to come this tenting among men would be especially impressive,'[8] we discover in the New Testament that Jesus is that better tabernacle.

A better temple

John continues to develop his tabernacle-temple theme as the gospel progresses. In the second half of chapter two, Jesus' concern for the purity of the temple, which he calls his father's house, provokes him to cleanse it of its sacrilegious practices. In doing so he shows great respect for the temple – but his actions also provoke a rather negative response from the Jewish leaders who demand a miracle as proof of his authority to perform such an action. Jesus' reply changed the focus of their concern from the material building to the God-man standing before them.

> 'Destroy this temple and I will raise it again in three days.' The Jews replied 'it has taken forty-six years to build this temple, and you are going to raise it in three days?' But the temple he had spoken of was his body. After he was raised from the dead, his disciples recalled what he had said. Then they believed the Scripture and the words that Jesus had spoken (John 2:19-22).

John's explanation is both helpful and interesting. Jesus is clearly referring to himself. He is the new temple who will be 'raised' in three days. After the resurrection the disciples believed what Jesus had said, understanding the scriptures which pointed to him.

But what scriptures were these? They must be those Old Testament texts which tell us about a new temple. It is possible that as no particular scripture is cited that Jesus had something else in mind, perhaps the vindication of the messiah.[9] But it is just possible that Jesus and the disciples after the resurrection were thinking about the wonderful picture of the new temple at the end of Ezekiel, from which a life-sustaining river would flow:

> The man brought me back to the entrance of the temple, and I saw water coming out from under the threshold of the temple . . . . this water flows towards the eastern region and goes down into the Arabah, where it enters the Sea. When it empties into the Sea, the water there becomes fresh. Swarms of living creatures will live wherever the water flows . . . so where the water flows everything will live . . . fruit trees of all kinds will grow on both banks of the river. Their leaves will not wither, nor will their fruit fail. Every month they will bear, because the water from the sanctuary flows to them. Their fruit will serve for food and their leaves for healing. (Ezekiel 47, extracts)

It could be that Jesus, as the new Temple, is the one from whom living waters would flow; the one who would sustain life and quench thirst. Certainly the presentation of Jesus in the gospel of John would lead us to such a conclusion. John's aim is to show the reader how to achieve eternal life through Christ[10] and it is therefore possible that when Jesus speaks of the living water in John 7 (which we have already thought about in connection with his provision) he is alluding to the new temple of Ezekiel's vision.

> If anyone is thirsty, let him come to me and drink.
> Whoever believes in me, as the Scripture has said,
> streams of living water will flow from within him.
> (John 7:37,38).

Undoubtedly these verses contain much Old Testament imagery and there has been some debate as how they should best be translated – did Jesus mean that living waters will flow from the believer (as in the NIV translation) or did Jesus mean that they will flow from him? The latter would support the case that Jesus is referring to himself as the new temple; the former that there is a consequence for the believer participating in the benefits of Jesus being the new temple.

Either way, associations can be made. Jesus is the new temple. He is the place where God would meet his people. Before we come to chapter 7 of John the readers of the gospel have been introduced to the fact that it would be in him, not in a building that the believer would find God. Not long after the bold and outrageous statement about the Temple in chapter 2, Jesus speaks with the socially outcast Samaritan woman. As with all Samaritans, their focus of worship was not the Temple in Jerusalem but on mount Gerazim. But Jesus says:

> Believe me, woman, a time is coming when you will worship the Father neither on this mountain nor in Jerusalem . . . a time is coming and has now come when the true worshippers will worship the Father in Spirit and truth. (John 4:21, 23)

Interestingly, Jesus also speaks in this chapter about the living water which comes only from him. The temple imagery is rich and deep. But it is at his death that this might be most clearly seen. In John we read of blood and water flowing from the recently deceased Jesus. Could the water here relate to the temple promise of Ezekiel? Even if it does not, the synoptics tells us that at the moment of Jesus' death, the curtain of the temple (separating the most holy place, the dwelling of God, from the rest of the temple), ripped in two from top to bottom. The most holy place is exposed; the barrier has been broken down. We can freely come to God.

Thus in the death of Jesus, the purpose of the temple finds its fulfilment. God no longer meets his people in a place but through a person. God no longer needs sacrifices, because the once-for-all final sacrifice has been made. And God no longer needs a mediatorial priest, because Jesus has fulfilled that function. It is therefore in the cross of Christ that the issues of the last three chapters – that of sacrifice, priest and temple, ultimately find their fulfilment. In Christ (and supremely in his death, according to John) we see the glory of God and through him we come to God. What a relief it is to know that we do not need to travel to a particular place (a temple) to meet a particular person (a priest) to find forgiveness. The answer lies in Jesus.

The perfect temple

One final issue relating to the temple needs to be discussed. Exodus leaves us with intricate instructions about an earthly sanctuary. Ezekiel leaves us with a wonderful vision of a perfect one. Jesus takes us from one to the other by being the fulfilment of the tabernacle and temple on earth – but there is yet more to come. The death of Jesus is a means to an end – and that end is the people of God gathered round the throne of God, glorifying the Lord in the new heaven and the new earth, where the old order has disappeared. There are no barriers; there is no sin. Heaven is perfect.

The writer to the Hebrews speaks of that heavenly sanctuary in that place of perfection. This is the sanctuary at which the Lord ministers as our great high priest[11] and 'into which Christians are invited to enter for their worship of God.'[12] The specific instructions of the Old Testament were in part to help us to understand the eternal tabernacle and the once for all sacrifice which enables us to approach the enthroned Lord without fear and free from condemnation.

All believers, Old Testament and New, find their salvation through Christ and his death – an eternal grace-gift that none of us deserves. But now that Christ has *physically* come and *physically* died, there is no need for the earthly tabernacle or temple. Indeed, there are now no holy places on earth, but thanks to the mercy of God, there is open access to the truly holy place of heaven.

So where do we meet God and how do we know God? In the person of Jesus Christ.

NOTES:

[1] *An Introduction to the Old Testament* Dillard and Longman (Apollos: Leicester,1995) Introduction p.70

[2] See 1 Samuel 4:4 and Psalm 99:1

[3] *An Introduction to the Old Testament* p.68

[4] Numbers 1 and 2 gives explanation as to how and where the different tribes were located.

[5] *The Symphony of Scripture* Mark Strom (P&R Publishing, 2001) p.64

[6] D.A Carson *The Gospel according to John* (Leicester:IVP, 1991) p.127

[7] *The Gospel according to John* I-XII (Doubleday, 1966) Raymond E. Brown John p.33

[8] Brown *John* p. 32 cf. Joel 3:17; Ezekiel 37:7

[9] D.A. Carson *John* p.183

[10] John 20:30.31

[11] See chapter Eight

[12] David Gooding *An Unshakeable Kingdom* (Leicester, IVP), p.180

10

A Better King (I)

We don't have to have been a Christian for very long before we realize that the person of Jesus is closely connected to the concept of kingship. Even the name we so happily use, that of Christ, is packed with Old Testament background and meaning. We could start there, picking up the familiar words of our Christian experience and exposing them to the light of Old Testament expectation, but it might be better to describe the stage before seeking to understand the drama that is played out upon it; to look first at that expectation and then to see how Jesus has fulfilled it in all he said and did.

We have seen already that Israel had a king. He made his dwelling in the tabernacle, encamped at the centre of his people. He led his people as they travelled, provided for them and protected them. Theirs was an unseen king, a divine king, who ruled this theocracy with perfection. As R.T. France has said, 'To be the people of God was to recognize God as their king.'[1] Small though they were as a nation, the God of Abraham, Isaac and Jacob had shown his power and his provision. He had rescued them from the imperial tyranny of Egypt and had promised them a land of their own. They would be his people, the vehicle of God's revelation to the world[2]. As such, their king was like no earthly king and their future more certain that the greatest and most powerful earthly dynasty.

But our story so far has shown that humanity is more fickle that we might hope. Like us, the people were crippled with the sin that was to pull them away from this king. As we read the pages of the Old Testament, we shall find that although an earthly king for this theocratic nation was to come, the motives with which the people would ask for this king would be driven not by their desire to serve God but by the pressure of the pagan nations that surrounded them.

A king for Israel

Deuteronomy 17:14-20 allows for the appointment of an earthly king. Any true Israelite would have known that God alone was the real monarch, the true king of Israel[3], but this legislation permits and recognizes that at some point in their future history, the people will want to appoint an earthly king. As such, God graciously spells out for them the nature of this kingship.

> When you enter the land the LORD your God is giving you and have taken possession of it and settled in it, and you say, 'Let us set a king over us like all the nations around us', be sure to appoint over you the king the LORD your God chooses. He must be from among your own brothers. Do not place a foreigner over you, one who is not a brother Israelite. The king, moreover, must not acquire great numbers of horses for himself or make the people return to Egypt to get more of them, for the LORD has told you 'You are not to go back that way again.' He must not take many wives, or his heart will be led

> astray. He must not accumulate large amounts of
> silver and gold. (Deuteronomy 17:14-17)

God had recognized that the people would ask for a king so that they could be like the other nations, even though they had agreed to be distinct from the other nations. They had been called to be, and had agreed to be, a holy and royal priesthood, the vehicle of God's purposes for the world. Never-the-less, in his sovereignty he legislates for their request. The earthly king must be God's choice and a brother Israelite. Unlike the kings who surrounded God's people, their king was not to mark his power by material possessions. For although 'military aggrandizement, a large harem and amassing of wealth were typical of Eastern potentates long before Moses' day,'[4] the people of God were driven and constrained by a different set of priorities. The restrictions placed upon the pattern of Israelite kingship 'cut across the accepted pattern of kingship throughout the Ancient Near East.'[5] Theirs was to be a king with a difference, divinely appointed and divinely accountable, whose greatness was not to be seen in the strength of his army, the magnitude of his wealth or the size of his harem, but in his faithfulness to the greater king who had appointed him to this godly office.

It is no surprise then that the king was expected to be diligent in his obedience to the law. True kingship was to be seen in his faithfulness to the covenant God.

> When he takes the throne of his kingdom, he is to
> write for himself on a scroll a copy of this law, taken
> from that of the priests, who are Levites. It is to be
> with him, and he is to read it all the days of his life
> so that he may learn to revere the LORD his God and
> follow carefully all the words of this law and these

decrees and not consider himself better than his brothers and turn from the law to the right or to the left. Then he and his descendants will reign a long time over his kingdom in Israel. (Deuteronomy 17:18-20)

Certainly by the time the people were in the promised land, the need for a king had become apparent. Only a king could remedy the political, moral and social collapse of Israel which we see at the end of the book of Judges[6].

1 Samuel 8

In 1 Samuel 8 the long expected request for a king is finally made. In God's great sovereignty he had recognized that Israel would request a king to be like the other nations and that in doing so they would, in effect, be rejecting the kingly rule of God himself. Samuel, displeased at the people's request, prayed to the Lord. And God said to him:

Listen to all that the people are saying to you; it is not you they have rejected, but they have rejected me as their king. As they have done from the day I brought them up out of Egypt until this day, forsaking me and serving other gods, so they are doing to you. Now listen to them; but warn them solemnly and let them know what the king who will reign over them will do. (1 Samuel 8:7-9)

The following verses spell out the kind of king the people will be given. He will indeed be like the kings of the other nations, acquisitive, powerful and feudal. But the people persist, wanting a king to lead them out and fight their battles like the kings of other nations.

How sad that the people of God had stooped so low. They had been promised land and blessings. They had a great king who had led them from slavery and through the wilderness and who had led them in victory. They had been given a land. But their request revealed their hearts – they were admitting that an invisible king was not enough. They still wanted to be like the pagan, godless nations around them rather than live as the glorious nation of God. As Goldsworthy has said, 'That the motives of Israel in asking for a king are all wrong can be seen in the nature of their expectations, which are political and military rather than truly religious. The request is seen as a rejection of God's rule.'[7]

Yet in the midst of that rejection we see the astonishing mercy of God. For the history of Israel from this point shows that God proceeds 'to make what they asked in unbelief into the primary and golden vehicle of his eternal purposes and blessings. His king would come and reign, a supreme gift of grace to an unworthy people.'[8]

Strange though it may seem, the institution of kingship is therefore both a rejection of the kingly rule of the creator, covenant God and a great gift from that same God, the means by which God would come and rule his people and rescue them from the sin that causes such rejection in the first place. We must therefore make a distinction between the kind of king requested and the nature of kingship which lay in the supreme and sovereign purposes of God.

Although there is risk of over-simplification, the first two kings in the history of Israel give us a model of the wrong kind of king and the right kind of king. Saul is the king chosen to meet the request of the people and later David is the king chosen to model the purposes of God.

Saul

Saul was God's answer to a request made with the wrong motives – the request of 1 Samuel 8. He was impressive in the world's eyes, tall, handsome and able – and as the chosen king he was anointed by God. But as that king he was also expected to meet the conditions of kingship as laid out in Deuteronomy. He was to be obedient to God and his law, a faithful example to the covenant community.

Instead, his disobedience led to his downfall: he did not utterly destroy the Amalekites as requested by God; he usurped the priestly prerogative of sacrifice; and finally, in desperation he consulted a medium.

By the middle of the book of 1 Samuel, Saul has been rejected as king in favour of David.

David

Unlike Saul, David was not a natural choice – he was young, inexperienced and had better qualified older brothers. But he was God's choice of king, a man after God's own heart, not the heart of the sinful people. So while 'Saul represented the folly of Israel's request, David represented God's choice and pattern of kingship.'[9]

David's accession to the throne was not straightforward. He was anointed king at Hebron by his own tribe, the tribe of Judah, and then remained 'at war' with the house of Saul. Throughout this time David never failed to recognize that Saul had been anointed by God. Despite Saul's rebellion and disobedience, David remained faithful, even though his life was constantly under threat. David trusted the God who had chosen him. Seven years later the other tribes acknowledged

David's kingship and one of the most famous kings of history began his reign.

At this stage the temple had not been built. God had travelled with the people in the tabernacle and although David secured the city of Jebus (renaming it Jerusalem, the city of peace) and restored the ark from its temporary residence in Kiriath-Jearim to the new capital city, there was no permanent dwelling place for God.

So David planned to build a temple, a house for God. But God had other ideas. He would build a 'house' for David. Not a physical dwelling – David already lived in a palace of cedar – but a dynasty, an eternal kingdom, through which God would bring about his purposes for mankind. The word of the Lord came to David through Nathan the prophet:

Now then, tell my servant David 'this is what the LORD Almighty says: I took you from the pasture and from following the flock to be ruler over my people Israel. I have been with you wherever you have gone, and I have cut off all your enemies from before you. Now I will make your name great, like the names of the greatest men of the earth. And I will provide a place for my people Israel and will plant them so that they can have a home of their own and no longer be disturbed. Wicked people shall not oppress them any more, as they did at the beginning and have done ever since the time I appointed leaders over my people Israel. I will also give you rest from all your enemies.

The LORD declares to you that the LORD himself will establish a house for you. When your days are over and you rest with your fathers, I will raise up your offspring to succeed you, who will come from

your own body, and I will establish the throne of
his kingdom. He is the one who will build a house
for my Name, and I will establish his kingdom
forever. I will be his father, and he shall be my son.
When he does wrong, I will punish him with the
rod of men, with floggings inflicted by men. But my
love will never be taken away from him, as I took it
away from Saul, whom I removed from before you.
Your house and your kingdom shall endure for ever
before me; your throne shall be established for ever.
(2 Samuel 7:8-16)

An eternal kingdom, rest from enemies, a place for God's
people. Here we have the ingredients for the chosen king
of God. David was humbled and heartened. God's
promise of land and blessings and descendants given to
Abraham all those years ago was now focused and fuelled
by the promise of an eternal kingdom given to King
David.

But why him? Was David any more special than Saul?
David was infamously disobedient with Bathsheba. He
committed adultery, then lied and finally committed
murder. Impressive though he was, he was also sinful
and imperfect. David wasn't a king because he showed
ability to be a king. David was a king because God had
chosen him to be a king. It was all grace. God would
fulfil his promises because he was God, not because
David was commendable.

And so David's reign was mixed. Although chosen
by God and anointed, he suffered years of persecution
before his accession to the throne; His misdemeanour
with Bathsheba caused yet further suffering and conflict;
the behaviour of his sons challenged his authority and
any popular notions of morality. David was a king in

receipt of the promise of God, but his reign was by no means a bed of roses. Maybe the people would see the promises reach their fulfilment in the reign of the next king – his son, Solomon?

Solomon

After the promise of 2 Samuel 7 many would have expected Solomon to be a great king. And in many ways he was. He asked for wisdom rather than power and built a temple for the Lord. The nation of Israel was reaching the peak of its power; the glory of God entered the Temple and the people rejoiced in prosperity and peace. Even the queen of Sheba, a representative of the pagan nations surrounding Israel, visited the king and marvelled at all she saw. By 1 Kings 10 we have a land, we have a people, we have a king, we have a temple, we have blessings.

But soon we have a king who has amassed 1400 chariots, 12000 horses (ironically imported from Egypt) and who made 'silver as common in Jerusalem as stones' (1 Kings 10:27). Almost all the conditions of kingship as given in Deuteronomy had been broken. The only one that remained was the instruction not to take many wives so that his heart would not be led astray. Then we turn the page to 1 Kings 11 . . .

> King Solomon, however, loved many foreign women besides Pharaoh's daughter – Moabites, Ammonites, Edomites, Sidonians and Hittites. They were from nations about which the LORD had told the Israelites 'You must not intermarry with them, because they will surely turn your hearts after their gods.' Nevertheless, Solomon held fast to them in love. He had seven hundred wives of royal birth and

concubines, and his wives led him astray. As
Solomon grew old, his wives turned his heart after
other gods, and his heart was not fully devoted to
the LORD his God, as the heart of his father David
had been. (1 Kings 11:1-4)

Solomon, who began with such hope, ended with such
horror. 'He was both the perfector of Israel's glory and
the architect of its destruction.'[10] During his reign Israel
had reached her zenith. By the end of his reign she was
heading for destruction. The great promises to David
were yet to find their fulfilment.

The kingdom after Solomon

Solomon's sin was the beginning of Israel's ruin. His
son Rehoboam provoked the division of the kingdom,
with the northern ten tribes refusing his kingship and
appointing Jeroboam to be their leader. Alternative
worship centres were set up at Dan and Bethel and a
golden calf was installed in each with the words 'It is
too much for you to go up to Jerusalem. Here are your
gods, O Israel, who brought you up out of Egypt.' (1
Kings 12:28). Jeroboam established the capital in Samaria
and married his son, Ahab, to Jezebel, a worshipper of
the god Baal. Soon the king and the people had turned
their back on their covenant God and pledged their
loyalty to Baal.

Disastrous king followed disastrous king. 'With each
new king, Israel hoped anew. He [Israel] hoped that this
one would be God's perfect messiah, the one who would
bring the golden age. Of each of its kings, Israel asked
"Are you the one who is to come, or shall we look for
another?" From the time of David onward Israel
expected a ruler who would save his people, a ruler who

would restore all the goodness of the creation.'[11] But it was not to be. Eventually the northern kingdom, known as Israel, was destroyed by the Assyrians in the eighth century BC. Many were deported and others intermarried. The ten tribes and the land they had occupied were relegated to the pages of history.

The Southern kingdom of Judah lasted for another 135 years until finally being besieged by Nebuchadnezzar in 598 BC. 3000 of the nobility were taken captive in Babylon and the temple treasures were removed. God's glory departed from the temple before it was finally destroyed in 587/6 BC after the vassal king Zedekiah had attempted to lead a rebellion against the Babylonians.

In all that time there had only been two kings who had followed the Davidic ideal. No 'son' of David was enthroned and there was no rest from their enemies. On the contrary, the city of peace, Jerusalem, had been destroyed. What had happened to the promises to Abraham and David? What of the land and blessings, the nation and the king? Where was God now that his glory had departed from the temple?

Such were the questions addressed by the prophets, those guardians of the covenant who had warned the people that they must repent and return to the God who had rescued them and made them his. God would not tolerate such rebellion. The judgement of the exile was God's punishment on an unrepentant people.

It could only be through the grace and mercy of that same God that forgiveness would come. Only the God of the promise could bring fulfilment of the promise. And from the ashes of the exile, through the word of those God raised as his spokesmen, there remained a glimmer of hope – a king would come, there would be a new temple and a new land, the exile would end. God would be God.

Psalms

We cannot leave this brief summary of the Old Testament teaching about kingship without at least a glance at the Psalms, where in so many ways the picture of kingship and the hope of this Messianic ideal find their expression. The brevity of this chapter will not allow for a thorough examination of the Psalms in question, but we can get a feel of the Messianic hope of kingship by looking at some selected highlights.

Psalm 2 indicates that the kings of the earth and the rulers of the world would take their stand against God's anointed one. This anointed one is of course none other than the Messiah, the Christ, God's son (Psalm 2:2,7). But that same anointed one would be victor by the grace and power of God, so much so that he would go on to 'rule the nations with an iron sceptre' and 'dash them to pieces like pottery.'

Psalm 45 picks up this picture of world rule, the rule of the one eternally blessed by God who would be pre-eminent among men, who would be concerned with morality and righteousness and would engender the praise of the nations. He would be divine himself and would rule with justice.

Psalm 72 reiterates many of these themes – the name of the Messiah will endure forever, nations will be blessed through him, righteousness will flourish under his rule. There will be prosperity and peace.

Psalm 89 tells us that he will be God's firstborn, the most exalted of the kings of the earth, the one to keep David's covenant.

Psalm 110 draws attention to his priestly function and his kingly rule even in the midst of his enemies.

Again and again we find reference to God's promised perfect king – a king for whom we search in the Old Testament with little success. The centuries pass and the promises stand but still no monarch emerges who will fulfil the promise and meet the expectation. But the people still wait in hope, through the trauma of the exile and the disappointment of their return to the land. A king must come – a 'son of man' who will rule with God-given authority over the nations. . . .

> In my vision at night I looked, and there before me was one like a son of man, coming with the clouds of heaven. He approached the Ancient of Days and was led into his presence. He was given authority, glory and sovereign power; all peoples, nations and men of every language worshipped him. His dominion is an everlasting dominion that will not pass away, and his kingdom is one that will never be destroyed. (Daniel 7:13,14)

A Davidic king, a divine son, a covenant keeper, the 'son of man' ruling with an everlasting dominion and power. Who would have thought that such a king would be born in the squalor of a stable in an occupied country? Who would have thought that this 'king' would fulfil the purposes of God by being crucified at the hands of those he had come to rule? Such is King Jesus, whom we have the privilege of calling 'Lord.'

NOTES:
[1] R.T. France *Divine Government* (SPCK, 1990). p.16
[2] Exodus 19:6

[3] Exodus 15:18; Numbers 23:21; Deuteronomy 33:5; Judges 8:23

[4] J.A.Thompson *Deuteronomy* (IVP,Leicester, 1974). p.205

[5] Christopher Wright, New International Biblical Commentary, *Deuteronomy*. (Paternoster,1996) p.209

[6] Judges 17:6; 18:1; 19:1; 21:25

[7] Graeme Goldworthy *Gospel and Kingdom* (Paternoster, 1981) p.71

[8] Alec Motyer, *Look to the Rock* (IVP, 1996) p.28

[9] Mark Strom *The Symphony of Scripture* (P&R Publishing, 2001) p.84

[10] Goldsworthy p.76

[11] P. and E. Achtemeier *The Old Testament Roots of our Faith* (SPCK, 1964) p.101

11

A Better King (ii)

The curtain of the New Testament raises to a stage already pregnant with anticipation. The scene has been set but the drama is far from its conclusion. We still await a king who will be obedient to the pattern laid out in Deuteronomy whilst also fulfilling the promise made to David and the expectations we read about in the Psalms.

All four gospels open with profoundly rich statements about Jesus, statements that leave us with the exciting reality that here at last is the long-promised king. **Matthew** begins with the potentially confusing genealogy which he tells us is a 'record of the genealogy of Jesus Christ the son of David, the son of Abraham.' (Matthew 1:1). Already we have seen the significance of this introduction with regard to the promises given to Abraham in the book of Genesis. Now we can add to it the wonder of the fulfilment of the promise given to David. 2 Samuel 7 promises that a son of David would rule forever on the eternal throne and over the eternal Davidic kingdom. He would be the Christ (or Messiah), God's anointed one – and Matthew 1 opens with the declaration that David's son, the promised king, has now come in the person of Jesus.

The genealogy further amplifies the wonder of the newly arrived king. Matthew tells us that there were fourteen generations from Abraham to David, fourteen from David to the exile and fourteen from the exile to Christ. This may be a significant pointer to Jesus as the Davidic king, for not only is the word 'David' represented by the number fourteen in Hebrew writing and thought, but we also see the genealogy sectioned into those periods of history which further confirm that Jesus is the long-awaited king. So Matthew takes us on an historical tour of the key moments in the history of Israel, which relate to Abraham, the father of the nation, to David, the one from whom the promised king of the nation would come and to the Exile, which was the catastrophic turning point in the understanding of the nation. Having read the first 17 verses of Matthew 1 we are left in no doubt that Jesus is the long awaited son of David.

Mark is equally direct in his account. He introduces Jesus as the Christ and the Son of God, the king of the kingdom. Again, as we read the pages of Mark we are left with a very clear impression that the king is here. The gospel takes us to the cross, but as it does so we are told that it is the Son of Man (picking up that wonderful phrase from Daniel and rich with kingly promise) who is to give his life as a ransom for many. The very king who miraculously reveals his divine hand in nature-transforming power is the one who is crucified as part of the kingship.

Luke provides a fuller account than Matthew of the events surrounding Jesus' birth. Mary's famous song, known by many as the Magnificat, praises God for what he has done and is about to do through the child soon to be born. So much of what Mary says reflects the messianic hope of the Old Testament – a hope focused on the king who would come. Then as the birth approaches, Mary and Joseph go to the town of Bethlehem, David's town, because Joseph is of the house and lineage of David. When he is born the angels announce that a saviour has been born, who is Christ the Lord. His birth is riddled with kingly associations.

John is even more astonishing in his presentation of Jesus. Jesus is the word – God himself, who comes and tabernacles among the people. It is just as the Psalm promises - the king is divine.

So at the outset of the gospels we are introduced to the long-promised king, an obedient king, who by word and action constantly confirms his identity. As the gospels unfold so the associations grow and the ultimate kingship of Jesus is displayed. A thorough survey would take us beyond the scope of this small book and so we shall have to restrict ourselves to a few thoughts. For even though 'kingship is one of the richest sources of our understanding of who Jesus is and what he has done,'[1] we can only touch on those sources to strengthen our understanding and fuel our praise. To that end I shall restrict my observations to one gospel, the gospel of John.

The gospel of John and the kingship of Jesus

The synoptic gospels (Matthew, Mark and Luke) tell us of the anointing of Jesus and the nature of his miracles – both of which confirm his kingship. Anointing is the means of distinguishing the monarch, and miracles identify the nature and the power of the kingdom of which Jesus is the king. In these two areas, John is different. There is no mention of Jesus' anointing, kingdom language only appears on two occasions and there are fewer 'miracles,' (which are commonly called 'signs' in John's gospel). These are carefully selected to give the reader a clear understanding that Jesus is the Christ, the Son of God. [2] Indeed, the whole purpose of his gospel is to so convince the reader of those truths that we might have faith in him – a faith which results in eternal life.

> These things are written that you may believe that Jesus is the Christ, the Son of God, and that by believing you may have life in his name. (John 20:31)

In his presentation of Jesus, John provides implicit and explicit confirmation that the king has come, the king in whom new life is possible.

Jesus as an obedient king

In the last chapter we looked at the conditions of kingship that had been laid down in Deuteronomy 17. The earthly king must be obedient in every way. He could not be a true king of Israel unless he recognized the Lord and submitted to his teaching. Obedience and faithfulness were to be the watchwords of the kings of Israel.

But any reading of the Old Testament and particularly of the history books (1 and 2 Samuel, 1 and 2 Kings, 1 and 2 Chronicles) reveals a catalogue of the sins and rebellions of the kings. The vast majority failed in every way, turning as they did from the true God to idols. And as they trusted in themselves rather than their creator and redeemer, so the nation plunged into dissipation and ruin. Not even Josiah and Hezekiah (the only great kings after David) could restore the nation's fortunes.

No king was up to the task, none of them truly fulfilled the Biblical conditions for an earthly king. We leave the Old Testament still searching for a king . . . . Until, that is, we open the pages of the New Testament. There we find a different kind of king, a true king, whose life was not marked by arrogance and pagan revelry, but by humble submission and obedience. There we find a king who 'sought none of the prerequisites of kingship, who gave himself to full and undivided allegiance to God, and who lives his whole life by the instruction, the torah, of the Lord.'[3]

Such allegiance is made clear time and time again in John's gospel. The intimacy of his obedience to God and determination to do his will run as arteries through the gospel:

> Jesus gave them this answer: 'I tell you the truth, the Son can do nothing by himself; he can do only what he sees his Father doing, because whatever the Father does the Son also does' . . . For I have not come down from heaven not to do my will but to do the will of him who sent me . . . The one who sent me is with me; he has not left me alone, for I always do what pleases him.' (John 5:19; 6:38; 8:29)

It is this obedience to his heavenly Father that finally took Jesus to the cross, mocked and crucified as a pretender, a false king, but dying to deal with the rebellion that characterized all previous kings and the people they sought to rule.

Jesus is a fulfilling king

John's presentation of Jesus is marked by a series of messianic declarations which both pick up the Old

Testament hope and also explain the New Testament fulfilment of kingship. Some are related to the 'I am' sayings[4], others confirm Old Testament expectation (such as the sign of the water into wine which picks up the Old Testament promise that the messianic age would be marked by the flowing of abundant wine.)

For our discussion, we shall look at just one example of the way in which Jesus demonstrates his kingship. In John 12 we read of Jesus' entry to Jerusalem on a donkey. His 'hour' has come and his death is fast approaching – this journey to Jerusalem will be his last. Famously, Jesus decides to ride on a donkey. At first sight this might seem to be a mark of humility, but John tells us otherwise. Humble though Jesus undoubtedly was, he chose this form of transport not to demonstrate his humility but his kingship. Jesus was clearly showing that he was the long awaited king of Old Testament prophetic hope.[5]

> Jesus found a young donkey and sat upon it, as it is written, 'Do not be afraid, O daughter of Zion; see, your king is coming, seated on a donkey's colt.' (John 12:14-15)[6]

At the time of his arrival in Jerusalem, the crowd clearly understood the significance of Jesus' actions. They were excited, longing for a deliverer to restore the land to its former glory. As it was the time of the Passover festival, national fervour was high. Excitedly the crowd cry out:

> Hosanna! Blessed is he who comes in the name of the Lord! Blessed is the king of Israel! (John 12:13)

Their cries contain so much hope and so much truth. But less than a week later we hear the cries of another crowd, perhaps even those who hailed Jesus as their king only a few days earlier. This time we find different words upon their lips. As Pilate presents Jesus with the words 'Here is your king,' the crowd shout out the chilling word - 'Crucify!' (John 19:15)

Jesus is a heavenly king

> Then Jesus declared, 'I am the bread of life. He who comes to me will never go hungry, and he who believes in me will never be thirsty . . . For I have come down from heaven not to do my will but to do the will of him who sent me. And this is the will of him who sent me, that I shall lose none of all that he has given me, but raise them up at the last day . . . Jesus said to them, 'I tell you the truth, unless you can eat the flesh of the Son of Man, and drink his blood, you have no life in you. Whoever eats my flesh and drinks my blood has eternal life, and I will raise him up at the last day.' (John 6:35, 38-39, 53, 54)

John 6 has provoked much debate, not least as to whether or not Jesus is speaking about the Lord's Supper when he referred to his flesh and his blood. Although it has often been taken in this way, a number of factors might lead us to think otherwise.

First, Jesus does not speak here of his body but of his flesh. Elsewhere in the New Testament the Lord's supper always contains reference to his body. *Secondly*, the context of the chapter would not lead those who first heard these words to make the connection with his sacrificial death. When we read of the Lord's supper in the other Gospels it is clear that Jesus institutes it at a Passover meal, when associations with sacrifice and redemption were already in place. At the Passover meal, bread was eaten and wine was drunk. The people were remembering the freedom that had been won for them when the lamb had been killed at the time of the Exodus. It was understandable in that context for Jesus to refocus the remembrance onto himself as the true lamb of God.

Thirdly, at the institution of the Lord's supper in the synoptics (Matthew, Mark and Luke) and in 1 Corinthians, Jesus is recorded as having used the familiar covenantal words of Exodus 24 which refer to the blood of the covenant, thereby doubling the association with his own death and explaining it clearly in Old Testament categories. These words do not appear in John's gospel. *Fourthly*, Jesus speaks elsewhere about an act of remembrance rather than the act of eating. *Fifthly*, John's gospel makes it clear that it is through faith, not ingestion of bread, that the believer is saved. (John 20:31). *Sixthly*, the very passage in which these controversial verses are contained states that the 'flesh counts for nothing' (6:63), which would be rather strange if he has been exhorting his followers to eat his flesh.

Finally, the wider context of the chapter suggests that Jesus is first and foremost speaking about himself. He has already said in 6:35 that it is by coming and believing (rather than eating and drinking) that salvation is possible. The chapter is therefore primarily Christological (about Jesus) rather than sacramental (about the Lord's supper). That much is made clear by the reaction of the crowd to Jesus and his subsequent response.

Their point of difficulty and disagreement with Jesus was his claim that he came from heaven. 'They said 'Is this not Jesus, the son of Joseph, whose father and mother we know? How can he now say, 'I came down from

heaven'?' (John 6:42). The crowd's concern is not bread
and wine, the significance of which they could not have
possibly understood at this stage, but the identity of
Jesus. He has just claimed that he is not earthly but
heavenly – the one who has come from the Father, full
of grace and truth. It is therefore his claim to divine
status and divine origin which cause many who hear to
question.

As Jesus continues to explain what he means, many
decide that it is too much . . . 'on hearing it, many of his
disciples said, 'This is hard teaching. Who can accept
it?" (6:60). They turn away because they cannot accept
that Jesus is the king from heaven. Only if Jesus returns
to heaven will his claims to divine and kingly status be
vindicated – so he says to them:

> Aware that his disciples were grumbling about this,
> Jesus said to them, 'Does this offend you? What if
> you see the Son of Man ascend to where he was
> before?' (John 6:61,62)

As he looks on the doubting and confused band of now
former followers he points out that it will be in his
resurrection and ascension that he will truly be seen for
what he is – the Son of Man (that wonderful phrase from
Daniel again) who will have all authority, power and
majesty in his heavenly and kingly rule. He has come
down from heaven to do his Father's will – and that
will is that everyone who looks to the Son and believes
shall have eternal life. Jesus is the king who stoops to
conquer.

Jesus is a proclaimed king

The trial of Jesus before Pilate is pulsating with dramatic tension. The Jewish leaders are on the 'outside,' both practically and spiritually. They have brought Jesus to Pilate with the sole intention of having him put to death. Pilate, on the other hand, is on the inside, questioning Jesus as to his identity and role and struggling to find a charge against him. The whole trial pivots on the issue of Jesus' kingship.

The first question Pilate asks Jesus is, 'Are you the king of the Jews?' We are given no information as to how or why Pilate should ask that question. Perhaps he was aware of the crowd's cries as Jesus entered Jerusalem; perhaps he was afraid of his own political position. We are not told. But it was a brilliant question to ask. Jesus responds by explaining the nature of his kingdom and therefore the nature of his kingship:

> Jesus said 'my kingdom is not of this world. If it were, my servants would fight to prevent my arrest by the Jews. But now my kingdom is from another place.' (John 18:36)

Jesus acknowledges and declares that he is a king, a divine king with the authority of God. As Pilate hears more about this man his determination to release him grows. On two occasions he goes out to the Jews and says that he finds no basis for charge against Jesus, the second of which brings this response from the Jews:

> We have a law, and according to that law he must die, because he claimed to be the Son of God. (John 19:7)

Now Pilate is really rattled and badgers Jesus to respond to his earthly protestations of power. But it is to no avail. Jesus simply tells Pilate that he would have no power over him were it not given from above. From that moment on, Pilate tries to free Jesus, faced as he is with the claims of Jesus as the king and the Son of God. He has been presented with the truth that John wants his readers to grasp as they understand the gospel. Here is Jesus, the Christ, the Son of God.

But the political pressure is too great. Outside, the Jews kept shouting 'If you let this man go, you are no friend of Caesar!' So Pilate brings Jesus out and presents him before them with the words: 'Here is your king.' It is at this point that the perversion of the human heart and the irony of the passage reach their zenith, for the Jews who should have no king but God cry out, 'We have no king but Caesar.'

There is nothing left for Pilate to do. He hands Jesus over to be crucified – but as he does so he insists that a sign be nailed on the cross with the words 'Jesus of Nazareth, the King of the Jews.' It is to be written in Aramaic, Latin and Greek, for all to see.

The Jews have rejected their king and sworn allegiance to the pagan emperor whilst Pilate has in some way acknowledged the king and proclaimed him to the world. There on the cross the king dies – raised up in death to raise up from death those who will believe in him. So the trial proclaims Jesus as the king and the Son of God. It takes him to the cross where the whole world may know who he is – Jesus of Nazareth, the king of the Jews.

Jesus is a risen king

John's gospel ends with two chapters which tell us about the resurrection of Jesus. Perhaps one of the most well-known resurrection passages is that of doubting Thomas, as it is commonly known. Thomas had not been with the disciples the week before when Jesus had appeared to them behind locked doors and he would not believe the testimony of the other disciples when they told him.

> Unless I see the nail marks in his hands and put my finger where the nails were, and put my hand into his side, I will not believe it.' (John 20:25b)

A week later the disciples were gathered in the house again. This time Thomas was with them. Once again Jesus entered the locked room. Looking at Thomas he said, 'Put your finger here; see my hands. Reach out your hand and put it into my side. Stop doubting and believe.' (John 20:27)

Thomas did not need to touch. He simply responded with the words 'My Lord and my God.' (John 20:28). That is the response Jesus wants us all to have. The king who died is the king who rose. More than that, he is the king who ascended to sit on the right hand of his father – the glorified Son of Man, who now rules and now reigns and before whom we must submit. The long awaited king has come. All hail king Jesus; all hail Emmanuel!

NOTES:
[1] Mark Strom, *The Symphony of Scripture* (P&R Publishing, 2001) p.90
[2] Scholars vary in their opinions as to what constitutes a 'sign' (the term used by John for his selected miracles),

but commonly assume there are between 6 and 9. The number is higher if the walking on the water, the resurrection and the miraculous catch of fish is included.

[3] Miller, *Deuteronomy: Interpretation*. A Bible commentary for teaching and preaching. (Louisville, John Knox, 1990) p.149

[4] A series of sayings in John's Gospel which reveal the identity of Jesus. They are connected to the self disclosure of God, as revealed at the Burning Bush in Exodus 3 when God said, 'I am who I am.' Other Old Testament associations are also apparent.

[5] This is also found in the synoptic gospels. Matthew 21:4-9; Mark 11:7-10; Luke 19:35-38

[6] Zechariah 9:9

12

A Better Answer

Any student of the Old Testament will know that is it very difficult to define prophecy. The office of the prophet emerged in a distinctive form with Moses, but it was not until the rise of the monarchy that prophecy became commonplace. These early prophets of God fought hard against the prevailing mindset that can be seen when one reads the history books of the Old Testament.[1] Mystical visionaries were to be found in all the religions of the day – some moved about in groups experiencing ecstatic utterances, others openly cut themselves in frenzy as they tried to bring about divine intervention of the gods they sought to serve.

The culture and the problems prophecy raised for the authentic believer were not so far removed from our present day – as mystic experiences and claimed divine utterances in the name of prophecy still confuse and perplex. The questions of how God speaks and through whom he speaks are ever real.

Certainly the prophets were regarded as the spokesmen of God, those entrusted with his words for the people. But prophecy was not simply about predicting the future or bringing 'new' revelation. It was more about explaining the character of God. After all, he had already revealed himself in his promises to Abraham, in the Exodus and the law given thereafter,

and later in the promises to King David. The prophets
were therefore covenantal spokesmen, guardians of the
truth, or 'watchdogs,' to use Goldsworthy's phrase[2].
Their message aimed to draw people back to the covenant
God in repentance and faith. They reminded people of
his truth, warned them of what would happen if they
did not repent (there would be judgement) and re-
emphasised what he had already done for them. Come
what may, he would be God – and the people needed to
know that however much they might protest otherwise,
nothing would stop the sovereign covenant God from
judging and saving.

As the monarchy spiralled further into depravity,
so the role of the prophet became more distinct from
the king and the people. They began to act out their
message and write it down. They were conscious of a
call from God and felt the burden of proclaiming his
message. They were often despised and ridiculed as
the people longed for a more pleasant message rather
than the warnings of judgement that often came from
their lips. Their audiences were largely religious
people – God's people, who knew the law and the
covenant, but who had remoulded their religion to
belittle sin, downplay judgement and encourage
syncretism.

So as we look at the prophets we see a message
from God for the people of the day. They did not
speak in a vacuum – they spoke to a sinful people in
the light of the revealed character of God.

It may be helpful to give a brief summary of the
prophets so that we can place them in their historical
context.

The Early Prophets

The first person in the Bible to be called a prophet was Abraham (Genesis 20:7) but it wasn't until Moses that the role of the prophet found its normative form. He was to be the standard by which all later prophets were measured. As with all true prophets, he was called by God and therefore stood before the people not with his own authority but as one who spoke God's words.

10th Century BC

The historical books (1 and 2 Samuel, 1 and 2 Kings) open with the call of Samuel – a 'seer' whose authority and prophetic office was recognised from 'Dan to Beersheba' (1 Samuel 3:20). Although the Lord had revealed himself to Samuel 'through his word,' the people to whom he spoke still turned away, wanting a king 'as all the other nations have' (1 Samuel 8:5) rather than accepting the authority of God, their true king, as revealed through the prophet.

As we have seen already, God granted their request and Samuel anointed Saul as the king of Israel. Interestingly, one of the signs experienced by Saul as a mark of that anointing was that he began to prophesy – a confirmation that the Lord had come on him in power and that he had been changed into a different person. (1 Samuel 10:5-7). The nature of this particular prophecy was what some have called ecstatic; Saul was caught up in a procession of prophets who were playing music and joined them in their 'prophecy.'

Whilst in this context it served as a confirmation of his office, we find prophecy appearing later in the book to prevent Saul's abuse of that same office. By 1 Samuel

16, the Lord has chosen David as king and the Spirit of the Lord has departed from Saul. Yet in chapter 19, Saul and his men, along with Samuel, are caught up in this ecstatic prophecy.[3]

It is difficult to explain the exact nature of this prophecy. Clearly God could use it for his sovereign purposes and clearly it was not impossible for the otherwise statesman-like Samuel to be caught up in it. But we also find such prophecy marked those who worshipped other gods and proclaimed another message (as with the prophets of Baal). The determining factor for authenticity is therefore more likely to relate to that which is consistent with God's truth. False prophets took the people away from their trust in the God of Abraham, Isaac and Jacob and from the law given to Moses; true prophecy brought people closer. Here, in the 10th century, this occurred either by speaking God's truth to the people (as with Samuel) or as a form of ecstatic prophecy which confirmed God's already spoken word (as with Saul). In both cases the end point was a desired conformity to God's will.

9th Century BC

The prophets of the ninth century still do not have the luxury of an eponymous book. But they are no less well known than their later associates. Elijah is found towards the end of the book of 1 Kings and at the beginning of 2 Kings. All but the last of the six episodes associated with his life related to the clash between Yahweh (the God we know from the scriptures), and Baal, the official protective deity of Tyre. It was through Jezebel, Ahab's wife, that Baal worship was introduced to Israel and it was through the prophet Elijah that God brought the people back to him.

Elijah holds a significant and important place in the scriptures. Not only does he fit within the pattern of Moses but also he is a forerunner of John the Baptist[4] and the prophets' representative figure at the transfiguration of Jesus.[5] As a prophet, he was almost alone as the mouthpiece of God, isolated yet protected, able to perform miracles in a land which had turned its back on the true God.

Elijah spoke to the people of the day as they rebelled against their true king and the pattern laid down for them in the Law of Moses – indeed, in some sense Elijah is another 'Moses' figure.[6] But at the same time he was just a man (James 5:17) who could not ultimately deal with the sin and rebellion of the people. Therein lies the problem of all the prophetic figures.

Elisha takes over the role and spirit of Elijah after Elijah's 'translation' to heaven. He too had powers given by God, but he too was unable to deal with the sin of the people to whom he ministered. Significant though Elijah and Elisha were, any response to their ministry was but a momentary relapse from the rebellion of the nation.

8th Century BC

The eighth century was a time of turbulence for the people of Israel. The Northern Kingdom, which had declared independence from King Rehoboam in the tenth century, now found its very existence under threat. Assyria was beginning to flex its political muscles whilst the increasingly godless kingdom of Israel was seemingly oblivious to the consequence of their idolatry and rebellion against their creator God. So God raised up prophets to warn of his impending judgement and proclaim his sovereign salvation.

Joel

Although difficult to date (and therefore perhaps not an eighth century prophet), Joel is a significant figure in Old Testament prophecy. He was the first prophet to use the phrase 'the day of the Lord' and looked forward to a time when God would pour out his Spirit on all people.

Jonah

Jonah did not prophesy to Israel (the Northern kingdom) or Judah (the Southern kingdom), but to Assyria, the very nation that would go on to threaten Israel's existence. The book reveals God's concern for the whole world, his sovereign control and his great compassion on sinful people. Jonah's reason for not wanting to preach to the people of Nineveh (the capital city of Assyria) was that he knew God to be full of compassion and did not really want those outside God's chosen nation to repent.

Hosea

Hosea enacts for us the faithfulness of God to a faithless people. Israel had turned her back on God in favour of a prosperous and idolatrous lifestyle. Such 'prostitution' necessitated a radical call back to God and hints of a 'new Exodus' for his people.

Amos

Amos speaks of the injustice and inequality which stemmed from Israel's perversion of the true faith. They still kept the outward trappings of Israelite religion, but their hearts were elsewhere. The Assyrians would act as God's judgement on the people, from which a remnant would be maintained, in accordance with the sovereign purposes of God.

Isaiah

Isaiah preached to the Southern kingdom of Judah and reassured King Hezekiah that in the 8th century, Jerusalem would not fall. Later the book addresses the situation after the fall of Jerusalem in the 6th century and presents a wonderful picture of messianic restoration, which includes a new heaven and a new earth.

Micah

Micah, as with many of the prophets, saw the social breakdown which arose from the sinful leanings of the people. Through his message we see that the Lord would maintain and fulfil his promises one day, ruling over the purified remnant of Israel.

7th Century BC

Nahum

Nahum prophesied against the Assyrian capital of Nineveh, leaving his hearers and readers with a picture of the Lord's total control over history. He would be the ultimate judge and king of all men.

Habakkuk

Habakkuk was prophesying as the Assyrians began to weaken. The Northern Kingdom of Israel had been destroyed. Now the Southern kingdom of Judah, centred on Jerusalem, was under threat by the Babylonian

Empire. She had not heeded the warnings of history and in almost gleeful abandon was indulging in the same godless lifestyle as had marked the northern kingdom before its destruction. Judgement awaited their folly. Trust in the sovereign God was the only answer.

Zephaniah

Zephaniah preached at the same time as Habakkuk and called for reform of the country and her ways whilst also announcing judgement. Through his prophecy we see a vision of cosmic judgement and salvation. This 'day of the Lord' was to be the long-awaited fulfilment of the promises made to Abraham hundreds of years before.

Jeremiah

Although he prophesied before the catastrophic events outlined below, Jeremiah is very much a prophet of the 'exile.' He knew that restoration of the institutions of the nation's religion would not be enough to avoid the forthcoming judgement and disaster. The temple, the sacrificial system, the ark of the covenant and the monarchy would not in themselves bring about renewal. The people had failed to grasp the enormity of their sin and the God with whom they were dealing. But through it all Jeremiah promises that God will maintain the covenant he had made with David and renew the covenant he made with Israel. He will raise up a 'branch from David' who would rule over a renewed Israel. This king would be very different to the ones ruling the physical land before its destruction by the Babylonians.

6ᵗʰ Century BC

The 6ᵗʰ Century witnessed the most devastating events in the history of Israel. The land was taken over and occupied, the glory of God departed from the temple and the city of Jerusalem was destroyed. Humanly, it looked as if God had abandoned his people. But from the ashes of the 'exile,' as it is called, from those 'saved' through God's judgement, there arose the focused hope of a messiah, God's king. He would fulfil the promises given to Abraham and David and would rule his people – and the world – with peace and justice.

Obadiah

Obadiah prophesied against the people of Edom (the descendants of Esau), just after the fall of Jerusalem in 587BC (some debate this and assume that the book is earlier). Despite the assault of God's enemies, God would rescue his people 'on the day of the Lord'.

Ezekiel

Ezekiel presents a powerful picture of the sovereign God – the one who will act because of his name. God promises to judge Israel and the nations. In doing so he will show that he is God. He will do it for the glory of his name. But because of that same name he would also save. Ezekiel promises a renewed people with a new leader in a new land enjoying life in a new temple, from which a river-sustaining life would flow.

Daniel

Daniel shows the activities of a faithful remnant of God's people in exile and reminds us afresh of the future rule of the sovereign Lord. God will establish an eternal kingdom through which 'one like the son of man' will demonstrate his total authority over all.

Post Exilic Prophets

The Old Testament closes with the writings of those prophets who emerged after the exile. Following a decree from Cyrus the Great of Persia, the people return to the land and slowly the temple is rebuilt, but it never achieves its former glory. Ezekiel's hope of a new temple is nowhere to be seen and the people, though chastised by their experience, fail to learn its lessons. So much of the prophetic promise remains unfulfilled.

Haggai

Haggai's objective was to encourage the people to complete the task of building the temple, which had run into disarray within a few years of their return to the land. Their apathy was spiritual in cause and practical in experience (drought and famine). The same promises of restoration to former glory and the hope of a Davidic king who would rule the people inspire the people to action.

Zechariah

Zechariah's ministry was concomitant with the people's return to Israel. His vision of the restored land includes the new temple with a consecrated high priest and a new people who would shine as light in a dark world. But in order to achieve this vision, the people must be purged of their guilt. The book concludes with the final victory of God's people and the arrival of their king.

Malachi

Malachi returns us to the old themes of a rebellious people. They had defiled the temple, intermarried, perverted the priesthood and caused social injustice. Once again, they were called to repentance. Their only hope lay in the character of the almighty God – the great day of the Lord would dawn, the godly would be destroyed and the righteous vindicated. And before all this happened, the prophet Elijah would return.

As we survey Old Testament prophecy, two aspects of Biblical truth come to the fore. The first is that humanity is sinful. Time and time again the prophets are required to speak because the people have turned their backs on their creator. They have a form of godliness but deny its power. They have a religion, but they have no fear of God. They have his words but fail to obey them. They have a responsibility to be God's holy nation and royal priesthood, but they turn to other nations and other gods. Prophecy reveals a faithless, sinful people.

Secondly, it reveals a faithful, righteous God. The covenant-keeping God will not ignore the covenant-breaking people. He will act because of his name, because he is God. He will bring a new order, a new Israel, a new Temple, a new covenant, a new heaven and a new earth; he will give his spirit and will provide a new shepherd to rule his renewed people.

In that sense Old Testament prophecy is about our Saviour. It does point to him. He is the answer to the problem of sinful humanity – and the one who brings God's ultimate judgement and salvation. But it does not point to him in a vacuum. Rather, God speaks to his people *then* – to remind them of his character and their need to repent; to tell them of the consequence of their actions. But in doing so he speaks to us *now*. We are given a greater picture of the gospel – God's gracious initiative which finds its ultimate fulfilment in Jesus. To that end prophecy has a double horizon. It spoke to the people of its day but it also points to the one in whom the solution to that day is found.

Jesus – The Fulfilment of Old Testament Prophecy

The Day of the Lord arrives
The Old Testament closes with the promise that God will send Elijah before the 'great and dreadful day of the LORD' (Malachi 4:5). The New Testament opens with the proclamation from the one whom Jesus identifies as that Elijah figure.

The message of John the Baptist is one of repentance from sins as a preparation for the coming Kingdom of God. Interestingly, the words he uses to make this proclamation are those associated with the restoration of God to his people. God will return. John is therefore the voice calling in the desert, 'Prepare the way for the Lord, make straight paths for him. (Matthew 3:3 quoting Isaiah 40:3).

When Jesus later speaks about John he explains his role as being the interface between Old Testament prophecy and the answer (or fulfilment) of that prophecy:

> For all the Prophets and the Law prophesied until John. (Matthew 11:13)

But in being the one who came before the Messiah and who prepared his way, he is also, according to Jesus, the promised messenger and Elijah figure of Malachi:

And if you are willing to accept it, he is the Elijah
who was to come (Matthew 11:14).

This explanation from Jesus provides us with a key to
understand the place of all Old Testament prophecy in
relation to Jesus. If John was the promised Elijah, then
he was the one who would come before the great and
dreadful day of the Lord. And by implication it means
that the coming of Jesus is the great Day of the Lord –
that long promised and long awaited time when God
would decisively act in the world with justice, judgement,
righteousness and salvation. It is this day which is so
keenly and universally awaited by the prophets of the
Old Testament – and it means that Jesus is the answer
to, and fulfilment of, all that has gone before.

The Fulfilment of Prophecy arrives

The Old Testament awaited a greater prophet, one like
Moses (as had been promised in Deuteronomy 18:15).
The crowd had already asked John the Baptist whether
he was that prophet but he had replied negatively[7]. In
some ways it was natural that their attentions might have
fallen to Jesus. He was born under difficult conditions
with the threat of a wicked king who attempted to kill
the future deliverer of God's people; he gave a 'new law'
on the 'mountain' as Moses had given the 'old law' at
Sinai. But it would be reading too much into the Bible
to assume that Jesus is simply the promised Moses
figure.[8] Although Jesus calls himself a prophet (Luke
4:24) and Christian history has often spoken of his office
of prophet alongside that of priest and king, Jesus is far
more. He is the fulfilment of both the law and the
prophets.

The New Testament is bursting with prophetic fulfilment, both directly and indirectly. The following references give no more than a taste of what rich pickings we have in the scriptures.

a) Matthew 5:17

> Jesus said, 'Do not think that I have come to abolish the Law and the Prophets; I have not come to abolish them but to fulfil them.'

Much ink has been spilt in attempting to work out exactly what Jesus meant when he said that he was a fulfilment of both the law and the prophets. In chapter five we attempted to look at the way in which the law points to Jesus and how it finds its fulfilment and continuing relevance in him. For the sake of our discussion in this chapter, we simply need to have the confidence that the prophets operate in the same way. I rather like D.A. Carson's summary of this rich and complex verse. 'The best interpretation of [this difficult verse] says that Jesus fulfilled the law and the prophets in that they point to him and he is their fulfilment.'[9]

b) Luke 24:25-27

> He said to them, 'How foolish you are, and how slow of heart to believe all that the prophets have spoken. Did not the Christ have to suffer these things and then enter his glory?' And beginning with Moses and all the Prophets, he explained to them what was said in all the Scriptures concerning himself.

How heartening it is to know that the first act of ministry in which Jesus engaged after he rose from the dead was to teach his disciples from the scriptures about himself.

How wonderful it would have been to hear his words! There is no doubt that Jesus sees the Old Testament as finding its fulfilment in him. He teaches from Moses and all the Prophets, which must include the law (as Moses is the lawgiver) and all the prophetic writings from Moses to Malachi.

c) Acts 10:42, 43

> [Jesus] commanded us to preach to the people and to testify that he is the one whom God appointed as judge of the living and the dead. All the prophets testify about him that everyone who believes in him receives forgiveness of sins through his name.

We have seen already that the prophets proclaimed the judgement and salvation of God. And here in the Acts of the Apostles, Peter proclaims that this judgement and salvation is to be found in Christ. He is the one of whom the prophets ultimately spoke.

d) Romans 3:21

> But now a righteousness from God, apart from the law, has been made known, to which the Law and the Prophets testify.

This is the first verse of what has been called 'Possibly the most important paragraph ever written.'[10] It speaks of how we can be right before God – declared as righteous and forgiven. By now we will have realized the importance of what that means and just what Jesus did to achieve it. How wonderful to know that this is what the prophets awaited. They testify to how we might be right before God through the Lord Jesus Christ.

e) Hebrews 1:1

In the past God spoke to our forefathers, through the prophets at many times and in various ways, but in these last days he has spoken to us by his Son, whom he has appointed as heir of all things, and through whom he made the universe.

Here the prophets are affirmed as the mouth-pieces of God. They were God's agents of revelation with the primary responsibility of bringing a wayward people back to their covenant responsibilities. Hebrews explains how that covenant has been fulfilled and superseded in the new covenant of Christ. As such, Jesus is God's 'final word.' Through him the conditions of the covenant are met and the punishment for sin has been removed. We are now free to approach the throne of grace with confidence. The hope of the prophets and the promise of God they proclaimed find their endpoint in Christ.

f) 2 Peter 1:19

And we have the word of the prophets made more certain, and you will do well to pay attention to it, as to a light shining in a dark place, until the day dawns and the morning star rises in your hearts.

It is fitting to close this chapter with the words of one of Jesus' greatest friends, Peter. He knew first-hand what Jesus was like and what he did. He knew of his teaching and of God's affirmation of his ministry on the mountain of transfiguration with Moses and Elijah. Peter knew what we need to know; that in Christ we have the word of the prophets made more certain. Jesus alone is the one in whom both the judgement and salvation of God find their fulfilment. He is the answer to all Old Testament prophecy.

NOTES:

[1] 1 and 2 Samuel, 1 and 2 Kings, 1 and 2 Chronicles

[2] 'All the prophets after Moses stand as the watchdogs of the society of God's people, working always within the framework of the covenant of Sinai.' Graeme Goldsworthy *Gospel and Kingdom* (Paternoster, 1981) p.78

[3] Samuel is rarely associated with ecstatic prophecy and may only have been so here because of the sovereign action of God.

[4] Matthew 11:14; 17:2

[5] Mark 9:4

[6] He returns to Horeb; he is succeeded by Elisha as Moses was succeeded by Joshua; God answers him with fire on two occasions (1 Kings 18:38; 2 Kings 1:10), which according to the Exodus narratives is representative of God's presence and judgement

[7] John 1:21

[8] 'The first two chapters of the gospel form a particularly striking manifesto on the subject of fulfilment, and in chapter two the Moses typology has a determinative place.' R.T. France Matthew – Evangelist and Teacher (Paternoster, 1989 (reprint 1992)) p.187

[9] D. A Carson *The Expositor's Bible Commentary*, Matthew 1-12 (Zondervan, 1995) p.143

[10] Charles Cranfield *A Critical and Exegetical Commentary on the Epistle to the Romans*, The New International Critical Commentaries (T. and T. Clark. Volume I, 1975) p.199

13

A Better Servant

We would not do justice to the Old Testament and its preparation for the coming of Christ without reference to the 'servant.' This image has been described as 'The most significant symbol in the Bible and in Christian religion.'[1] As we grasp its significance, so once again we are propelled into a deeper understanding of the one who came not to be served but to serve and to give his life as a ransom for many. (Mark 10:45)

Moses and David

Although the title 'servant' is applied to the recipients of the covenantal promises (Abraham, Isaac and Jacob)[2] early in the Bible, its usage becomes widespread as God himself designates Moses and later David as his *servants*. Moses is frequently referred to as a servant after his death, perhaps recognizing his special status amongst the people – God had communicated with him face to face. He alone had been chosen to lead the people of God out of their slavery in Egypt and he alone had been the one through whom God had delivered his law to the people. This role as God's servant is then passed to Joshua, the title also finding more common associations with his ministry after he had died.[3] In that sense, the book of Joshua is 'framed by references to the death of two supreme servants of Yahweh [God], whose lives are marked by humble and obedient service for him.'[4]

There is a subtle change in the use of the title as ascribed to David. Rather than being described as God's servant predominantly after death, David is frequently referred to as God's chosen servant during his lifetime. He alone is God's king, set over God's house and God's kingdom. And it is because God had promised to uphold David's line that later he acts in mercy towards his rebellious people – it is 'for the sake of my servant David' (eg. 1 Kings 11:13,32) that he will act. It is this promise to David that will survive the exile. From the ashes of the destruction of Jerusalem the prophets affirm the perfect rule of the Davidic servant king. Under him the people will live in peace and obedience.

Interestingly, the prophets themselves are also referred to as the servants of God, particularly the early prophets such as Samuel (1 Samuel 3:9) and Elijah (1 Kings 18:47). So by the time we arrive at the later prophets, there is already something of a stream of teaching: God's servants receive and continue the covenant; receive and give the law; rule as king and speak as prophets. From what we have read in the previous chapters, we may already be alert to what lies ahead – for Jesus is the one who brings the new covenant with its new 'law.' He is the one who fulfils all prophecy as the long-awaited Davidic king. The form of Jesus, the perfect servant, is already on our horizon.

The servant and the Book of Isaiah

Many of those who are reading this book will be familiar with Isaiah's image of the servant, not least because of those wonderful words from Isaiah 53 which have become for many a familiar part of Old Testament teaching.

It was towards the end of the nineteenth century that four passages in the book of Isaiah were identified as the 'servant songs.'[5] Since then the role and identity of the servant have been questioned by many, but as we look at the Old Testament in connection with the New, we will see that he is none other than Jesus, 'God's chosen servant, the one on whom God has poured out his Spirit with a specific mission on earth.'[6]

Isaiah 42:1-4

> Here is my servant, whom I uphold, my chosen one in whom I delight; I will put my Spirit on him and he will bring justice to the nations. He will not shout or cry out, or raise his voice in the streets. A bruised reed he will not break, and a smouldering wick he will not snuff out. In faithfulness he will bring forth justice; he will not falter or be discouraged till he establishes justice on earth. In his law the islands will put their hope.

Isaiah has already made it clear that the pagan gods are as nothing. And so the servant is introduced as the one who will bring justice and judgement to the whole earth. At this stage it is not clear who this servant might be. Although an earlier reference makes the nation of Israel a promising candidate (41:8), it is also apparent that the nation is spiritually blind (42:19), spiritually insensitive (42:20,25) and unfit for the task (42:22).

A 'better servant' is required – one who will fulfil Isaiah's expectations and in whom true justice is found. When we turn to Matthew's gospel it is this very passage from Isaiah that is used to explain the action of Jesus. (Matthew 12:15-21).

Isaiah 49:3-6

> He said to me, 'You are my servant, Israel, in whom I will display my splendour.' But I said, 'I have laboured to no purpose; I have spent my strength in vain and for nothing. Yet what is due to me is in the LORD's hand and my reward is with my God.' And now the Lord says – he who formed me in the womb to be his servant to bring Jacob back to him and gather Israel to himself, for I am honoured in the eyes of the LORD and my God has been my strength – he says, 'It is too small a thing for you to be my servant to restore the tribes of Jacob and bring back those of Israel I have kept. I will also make you a light for the Gentiles, that you may bring my salvation to the ends of the earth.

This second appearance of the servant finds him with a re-written job description. Now the mission of the servant is clarified both in his identity as a single person (so as to confirm the true servant is not the nation of Israel) and also in his ministry to the Gentiles. Israel as a nation has failed. God must now raise up this better servant to bring his mission to the world. In that sense 'the giving of the name to the servant here surely reflects the prophet's discovery that Israel in exile is not really capable at that moment of living up to what it means to be Israel.'[7]

Isaiah 50:4-9

> The Sovereign LORD has given me an instructed tongue, to know the word that sustains the weary. He wakens me morning by morning, wakens my ear to listen like one being taught. The Sovereign LORD has opened my ears, and I have not been rebellious; I have not drawn back. I offered my back to those who beat me, my cheeks to those who pulled out my beard. I did not hide my face from mocking and spitting. Because the Sovereign LORD helps me I will not be disgraced. Therefore have I set my face like flint, and I know I will not be put to shame. He who vindicates me is near. Who then will bring charges against me? Let us face each other! Who is my accuser? Let him confront me! It is the Sovereign LORD who helps. Who is he who will condemn me? They will all wear out like a garment; the moths will eat them up.

Unlike the city of Jerusalem and the nation of Israel, the servant is obedient and becomes an example to all who lead godly lives. But there is a cost to his faithfulness and obedience. That cost is suffering. In the verses that follow, the choice is put before the rebellious nation of Israel. Will they follow the servant and trust in the name of the Lord or will they 'walk in the light of their own fires' (50:11) which results in nothing but torment?

The true identity of the servant is coming into sharper focus. It 'begins to clarify and become more like Jesus.'[8] And as the identity of the servant becomes clearer, so does the choice presented to all who are confronted by the claims of Christ.

Isaiah 52:13-53:12

We now move into what is familiar territory for most Christians – the glorious and humbling picture of the sacrificed servant. Although it may be well known, it pays to be quoted in full.

> See, my servant will act wisely; he will be raised and lifted up and highly exalted. Just as there were many who were appalled at him – his appearance was so disfigured beyond that of any man and his form marred beyond human likeness – so will he sprinkle many nations, and kings will shut their mouths because of him. For what they were not told they will see, and what they have not heard, they will understand.

> Who has believed our message and to whom has the arm of the LORD been revealed? He grew up before him like a tender shoot, and like a root out of dry ground. He has no beauty or majesty to attract us to him, nothing in his appearance that we should desire him. He was despised and rejected by men, a man of sorrows, and familiar with suffering. Like one from whom men hide their faces he was despised ,and we esteemed him not.

> Surely he took up our infirmities and carried our sorrows, yet we considered him stricken by God, smitten by him and afflicted. But he was pierced for our transgressions, he was crushed for our iniquities; the punishment that brought us peace was upon him, and by his wounds we are healed. We all, like sheep, have gone astray, each of us has turned to his own way; and the LORD has laid on him the iniquity of us all.

He was oppressed and afflicted, yet he did not open his mouth; he was led like a lamb to the slaughter, and as a sheep before her shearers is silent, so he did not open his mouth. By oppression and judgement he was taken away. And who can speak of his descendants? For he was cut off from the land of the living; for the transgression of my people he was stricken. He was assigned a grave with the wicked and with the rich in his death, though he had done no violence nor was any deceit in his mouth.

Yet it was the LORD's will to crush him and cause him to suffer, and though the Lord makes his life a guilt offering, he will see his offspring and prolong his days, and the will of the LORD will prosper his hand. After the suffering of his soul, he will see the light of life and be satisfied; by his knowledge my righteous servant will justify many, and he will bear their iniquities. Therefore I will give him a portion among the great, and he will divide the spoils with the strong, because he poured out his life unto death and was numbered with the transgressors. For he bore the sins of many, and made intercession for transgressors.

There is much that could be said about these wonderful words. When the Ethiopian eunuch was travelling from Jerusalem to Gaza reading this passage of scripture, we are told that Philip 'began with that very passage of Scripture and told him the good news about Jesus.' (Acts 8:35); when Peter, who knew Jesus so well, writes about his character and his death he twice uses this passage, explaining the perfect character of Jesus and the nature of his death (1 Peter 2:22,24); when Jesus himself stands trial his silence enrages his accuser. He is the innocent one, the one who is as a lamb going to the slaughter. He is the one who dies voluntarily as the obedient substitutionary sin-bearer, the one who loves again to clothe the people with God's righteousness. Indeed, he is the only one who can perform that function, because he is the only one with the moral perfection to bear sins on behalf of others.

As we read on from this fourth servant song we see that 'Zion is called into a covenant of peace (54:10) and the whole world into an everlasting covenant (55:3).'[9]

The pages of the New Testament and the Jesus they present, rest firmly on these servant songs. Jesus showed perfect obedience in his ministry, humble and silent acceptance of his suffering in his death and thereby acted as the substitutional sin-bearer of the whole world. Where Israel failed because of their disobedience, Jesus succeeded. In being that 'better servant' he fulfilled 'all righteousness' and enabled people like you and me to stand before a holy God free from the condemnation of our sin. In his life he gave us the model of servant living and in his death he gave us a means of servant living, so that with others who have responded with faith, we can have that new life of the Spirit, a life which can begin before we die, but a life which takes us through death into his glorious presence. There we shall see the one who is the king, lamb, the servant, who is worthy of our praise now and for all eternity.

He did not consider equality with God something to be grasped, but made himself nothing, taking the very nature of a servant, being made in human likeness. And being found in appearance as a man, he humbled himself and became obedient to death – even death on a cross! Therefore God exalted him to the highest place and gave him the name that is above every name, that at the name of Jesus every knee should bow, in heaven and on earth and under the earth, and every tongue confess that Jesus Christ is Lord, to the glory of God the Father. (Philippians 2:6-11)

NOTES:

[1] John Mackay, *The Form of a servant.* Theology Today 15, 1958-1959, 304

[2] Genesis 18:3; 24:14; 26:4; 32:4,18; 50:17

[3] Joshua 24:17; Judges 2:8

[4] *Dictionary of Old Testament Theology and Exegesis* Volume 4 (Paternoster Press, 1996) p.1191

[5] B. Duhm 1892

[6] D.A. Carson *The Expositor's Bible Commentary* Matthew 1-12 (Zondervan, 1995) p.286

[7] J. Goldingay *God's Prophet* (Paternoster Press, 1984) p.128

[8] Philip Hacking *Discovering Isaiah* (Crossway Books, 2001) p.140

[9] Alec Motyer *The Prophecy of Isaiah* (IVP,Leicester, 1993) p.423

14

A Better Way

For no matter now many promises God has made,
they are 'yes' in Christ. And so through him the
'Amen' is spoken by us to the glory of God.

2 Corinthians 1:20

This chapter aims to be a summary of all that has gone
before. We have swept through the panoramic scenes of
God's activity in the Old Testament touching, often only
lightly, on the events and promises which find their
fulfilment in Christ. As Paul Barnett has written of the
above verse from 2 Corinthians: '[Christ is] the
fulfilment of all the promises of God made under the
old covenant, and thus of that covenant in its entirety;
no promise remains unfulfilled. 'In him' God has spoken
his 'yes.' His fulfilment is absolute, dimming whatever
glory there had been in the old covenant. Those who
are 'toward' him have the Spirit; those who are 'in him'
have 'become the righteousness of God' and are 'the new
creation' . . . . If Christ is God's 'yes' he is the church's
'Amen."[1]

The strength with which we say that 'Amen' will be
proportionate to the depth of our understanding of all
that has gone before. Jesus was no after-thought in the
purposes of God. From before the foundation of the
world, he was the purpose of God. All the promises, all

the history, all of what we read in the Old Testament finds its answer in him. All salvation is in him; for those awaiting his arrival 'in the flesh' and for those who now live after he has been 'in the flesh.' We are all dependent on the gracious initiative of God as seen in Christ. He is the alpha and the omega, the beginning and end. He is the Lord of all, the answer to life.

A Better Adam

Where Adam failed by being disobedient, Jesus 'succeeded.' And as Adam took humanity to the pit by his rebellion against God, so those in the pit can find their redemption in the 'second Adam' who was obedient to God.

A Better Son

God made a promise to Abraham which was confirmed through his sons. The hope of the promise was centred on Isaac, but only found its true fulfilment in the person of Jesus. The promised land, the promised descendants and the promised blessings can only be found in Christ. He is the 'seed' to which the promises to Abraham pointed.

A Better Passover

God rescued the people from their slavery in Egypt by the sacrifice of a lamb. Its death protected the people from the angel of death, the agent of God's judgement. The people were free to be God's people. In the same way, Jesus was the perfect Passover lamb, shedding his blood so that we might be free from the slavery of sin, free to be God's people and to go to his promised land.

A Better Covenant

God made an agreement with the people in the wilderness. Having rescued them as his people he then showed them how to live as his people. They agreed to keep the covenant on pain of death. But they failed. Thereafter we have the problem of a covenant-breaking people and a covenant-keeping God – a problem which only finds its fulfilment in Christ.

A Better Law

God gave the people law so that they would be a holy nation and a royal people. They were formed by the law, but they were also failed by the law. Sin prevented obedience. Jesus fulfilled the law and instructed those who have new life in him how they should live as God's people.

A Better Provision

As the people journeyed in the wilderness, God provided them with food and water, both to satisfy their needs and to test their faith. Jesus sustains us spiritually as we 'travel' to heaven. Faith in him is all we need.

A Better Sacrifice

God instituted a system of sacrifices which were required to deal with sin and restore the people's relationship with God. But all sacrifices were insufficient in that they needed to be repeated year after year. The absolute forgiveness of sins, and therefore free access to God, was not possible. Only in the death of Jesus do we find a sacrifice which is sufficient for all sin and therefore only in Jesus do we see the end to all sacrifices.

A Better Priest

In the Old Testament a priest was required to perform the sacrifice on behalf of the people. He was their mediator and intercessor, but his function was limited by his own sin and the inadequacy of the sacrifice. Only a perfect priest could make a perfect sacrifice and offer constant access to God. Jesus is that perfect priest.

A Better Temple

The temple and the tabernacle before it, was the dwelling place of God on earth. At its heart was the most holy place, ornately decorated and filled with the glory of God. The only person who could enter that holy place was the high priest, and then only once a year after he had offered sacrifices for his own sin. God was among the people but distant from the people. When Jesus died, the curtain to the most holy place was torn in two, from top to bottom. Now free access and permanent access is possible through Jesus. He is now the place where God meets his people.

A Better King

God was the true 'king' of the people. But in their rebellion they asked for a king to be 'like the other nations.' God granted their request, with disastrous results before appointing his own choice of king, chosen not because of merit but because of the purposes of God. These purposes find their fulfilment in the true king of Israel, the Lion of the tribe of Judah, Jesus himself.

A Better Answer

As the monarchy spiralled into depravity, prophets emerged urging repentance and highlighting the consequence of continued rebellion. God would judge – but in his mercy he would also bring salvation. Their message of restoration and fulfilment of the promises of God only finds its complete answer in Jesus.

A Better Servant

Whilst certain key figures in the Old Testament were designated with the title of 'servant,' the book of Isaiah looked for a perfect servant, obedient in all he did and therefore qualified to bear the sin of others and bring justice to the world. That servant is none other than Jesus Christ, the perfect and obedient son of God, the fulfiller of the hope of the nation of Israel and the one who would become a light to the Gentiles.

NOTES:

[1] P. Barnett NICNT *The Second Letter to the Corinthians* (Eerdmans, 1997) p.109

Epilogue

For some this book may have been too short, for others it may have been too long. By necessity it has been selective in the material chosen and brief in the topics studied. As I have written I have been humbled afresh by the Lord of whom the scriptures speak – the great Lord of glory, the enthroned king, the one for whom and through whom the world came to be and for whom we live (1 Corinthians 8:6; Colossians 1:15-20), yet the one who, though he was rich, yet for our sakes became poor, so that through his poverty we might become rich (2 Corinthians 8:9).

This book will have achieved its purpose if those who have read it then go on to read the Bible with renewed assurance, certainty and joy and above all, delight in the one of whom it speaks, our Lord Jesus Christ.

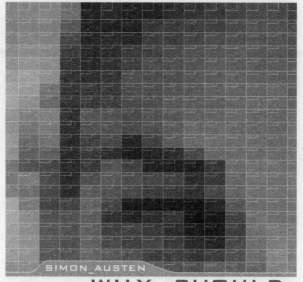

SIMON_AUSTEN

WHY_SHOULD GOD_BOTHER WITH_ME?

CHRISTIANITY_FRESHLY_EXPLORED

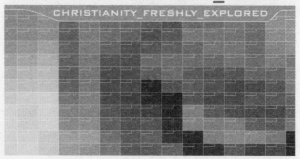

Why Does God Bother With Me?
Christianity Freshly Explored
Simon Austen

The modern secular viewpoint leaves us as insignificant walking monkeys who got a lucky evolutionary break. Nothing we do matters. If you are investigating the Christian faith the question 'Why should God bother with me?' is one that needs an answer.

An accessible, engaging and comprehensive explanation of the Christian faith, which I thoroughly recommend.
Rico Tice, Christianity Explored

If you are looking for a clear, straightforward explanation of the basics of Christian belief, in everyday language, this is your book. It is lucid, honest, illuminating and very readable!
David Jackman, The Proclamation Trust

Shrewd, sane and sensible, I wish this book every success. By success I mean that those who at present don't bother with God will read it and discover that God bothers with them.
Dick Lucas, The Proclamation Trust

A highly readable and very useful introduction to Christianity.
Alister McGrath
Professor of Historical Theology, Oxford University

Part C. S. Lewis, part John Stott, Austen invites conversation with unbelievers. God has in fact bothered with us more that we know.

Dr Mike Horton
Westminster Theological Seminary, California

ISBN 1 85792 719 2

"... a message the church needs to hear." R.C. SPROUL

REVEALING JESUS as
MESSIAH
Identifying Isaiah's Servant of the Lord'

Stuart Sacks

Revealing Jesus as Messiah
Identifying Isaiah's Servant of the Lord
Stuart Sacks

The Messianic Songs of Isaiah have been called the 'Fifth Gospel' – Why?

Stuart Sacks, Jewish believer, musician, author and broadcaster shows us how these fascinating sections of the prophecy of Isaiah point to one person as the Jewish Messiah.

Stuart Sacks brings the prophet Isaiah and his message to our day. It is a message that church needs to hear.

R C Sproul

In thirteen short, readable chapters Sacks provides insight into the nature and work of Jesus as Israel's and our Messiah and offers encouragement for those who want to know him and be like him. It would be difficult for anyone to read this book and not be helped by it.

James M Boice

Every generation needs good guides to key portions of the scripture, and the Servant Songs of Isaiah, often referred to as the 'fifth gospel', are surely fundamental to our understanding of the person and work of the Messiah. Stuart Sacks, a Jewish believer, has provided a very accessible guide to the significance and application of these crucial passages. His Jewish insights are woven into the text of the book in an easy manner. I heartily recommend it.

Walter Riggans
Church's Ministry among Jewish People

The author's ability to move fluidly between the promises and prophecies of Isaiah and their New Testament fulfilment makes this an enlightening and practical book. Clearly Stuart Sacks is thrilled to introduce to us his Messiah, and to encourage us all, Jew and Gentile alike, to know him....

John Ross, Christian Witness to Israel

ISBN 1 85792 311 1

Christian Focus Publications
publishes books for all ages

Our mission statement –

STAYING FAITHFUL
In dependence upon God we seek to help make His infallible word,
the Bible, relevant. Our aim is to ensure that the Lord Jesus Christ
is presented as the only hope to obtain forgiveness of sin, live a
useful life and look forward to heaven with Him.

REACHING OUT
Christ's last command requires us to reach out to our world with
His gospel. We seek to help fulfill that by publishing books that
point people towards Jesus and help them to develop a Christ-
like maturity. We aim to equip all levels of readers for life, work,
ministry and mission.

Books in our adult range are published in three imprints.

Christian Focus contains popular works including biographies,
commentaries, basic doctrine, and Christian living. Our children's
books are also published in this imprint.

Mentor focuses on books written at a level suitable for Bible College and seminary students, pastors, and other serious readers.
The imprint includes commentaries, doctrinal studies, examination of current issues, and church history.

Christian Heritage contains classic writings from the past.

For a free catalogue of all our titles, please write to
Christian Focus Publications
Geanies House, Fearn,
Ross-shire, IV20 1TW, Scotland

info@christianfocus.com